C000174388

FOUNTAINS OF ROME

FOUNTAINS OF ROME

Photographs by
Francesco Venturi

Text by
Mario Sanfilippo

TAURIS
PARKE
BOOKS

Note to the reader

This is what is known as a photographic volume d'auteur, in the sense that the fountains featured here were all chosen by the photographer, Francesco Venturi, who has captured those that particularly attracted his attention, choosing the angle and moment of day for each one. The accompanying introduction and outlines written by Mario Sanfilippo are merely to provide a framework and commentary, case by case, to accompany the photographer's personal choice.

Those who are familiar with the vast historiography on the three cities of Rome, know full well that water and fountains are ever-present in the historical events and unfolding stratification of the city's fabric. They will also know that the fountains have been dealt with in an infinite number of books, essays, articles, and photographic albums. One in particular is the work of Cesare D'Onofrio, who spent over thirty years carefully reworking his celebrated book; then there is another excellent volume by Bruno Brizzi. In the meantime, Willy Pocino has been busy preparing an authoritative inventory of the fountains of both past and present eras, and his list has apparently already reached the figure of 1,300.

In conclusion, the introduction and individual descriptions are the work of a "thief," someone with the ability to listen to those who have real knowledge of the subject, and borrow their thoughts. My main debts are listed in the meager bibliography at the end. By rights, the list should have been a mile long, but instead only the works of certified usefulness to the general reader have been cited, rather than those for specialists.

M.S.

For Allegra
Very special thanks to Filippo Del Drago, a helpful assistant and great cicerone, always full of ideas. It is because of him that this book came into being, after something he said one morning while we were admiring Bernini's Barcaccia fountain: "Why don't you write a book on the fountains of Rome?"
And to Celia and Allegra – one big, one small, both loved.
F.V.

The authors and editors wish to thank the archive department of the A.C.E.A. and its director Fabrizio Crespi for permission to reproduce photographs of the Peschiera terminus and the ornamental fountain of the Peschiera-Capore water corporation.

Published in 1996 by
Tauris Parke Books
An imprint of I.B. Tauris & Co Ltd
Victoria House
Bloomsbury Square
London WC1B 4DZ

Copyright © 1996 Amilcare Pizzi S.p.A.
Cinisello Balsamo (Milan)
Design and layout: Paolo Regini
Translated from Italian by Andrew Ellis

All rights reserved. Except for brief quotations in a review, this book, or any part of it thereof, must not be reproduced in any form without permission in writing from the publisher.

A full CIP record of this book is available from the British Library

ISBN 1 86064 146 6

Printed and bound in Italy

CONTENTS

THE SOCIAL USES
OF WATER
IN THE
THREE CITIES OF ROME

FOREWORD

Not yet out of their swaddling clothes, the babies Romulus and Remus were ordered by the usurper Amulius to be cast into the waters of the Tiber. Amulius' slaves were unable to reach the main river currents because the typical seasonal spate had flooded the narrow cleft that ran below the Capitol, Palatine, and Aventine hills. The slaves therefore left the twins in a basket amid the marshy river banks, convinced that as the swamp water withdrew it would take the sons of Rhea Silvia and the god Mars with it, thereby eliminating two undesirable pretenders to the usurper's throne. As a result, in traditional lore the history of the city is closely tied to water as having secured the salvation of its mythical founder.

To tell the truth, the legend tends to be a poetical cover-up of the unadorned fact that the city enjoys a very unusual geographical situation and topography: Rome was born alongside a ford, whose site lies immediately downstream from Tiber Island.

From its earliest beginnings, Rome enjoyed a special relationship with water, that indispensable element of human life, and of collective life in particular. Undoubtedly, this special relationship existed from the outset, from the times of the first settlements and villages on the hills. But the continuity of city life does not rule out the existence of three distinct cities of Rome.

The image down through time – first of the scattered villages perched on the various hillsides in the fourteenth century B.C., then the *urbs quadrata* of the eighth century B.C., the Rome of the monarchies (and especially the "Grande Roma" of the Tarquinii), and the ensuing sequences of republican and imperial Rome and the Rome of late antiquity – cannot be severed from the idea of geographical *position*, and the sense of *site* afforded by the topographical feature of the river.

The excellent geographical and topographical position of the city has always been the key to its exceptional development. Rome achieved a prosperity unmatched in Europe, though in the thirty-four centuries of the city's history the population and extension swelled and shrunk dramatically.

The ancient city progressed from the few hundred or thousand souls occupying a fortified precinct that began with the fabled sixteen hectares of Romulus' *urbs quadrata*, to a population of over a million inhabiting a built-up area covering an astonishing 1,400 hectares of land in the first centuries A.D.

The dire political and economic straits that followed the crumbling of the Empire were aggravated by a series of disastrous events, including the raids perpetrated by the Visigoths and the Vandals, the disintegration of the state institutions, the terrible burden of the protracted Byzantine-Gothic wars, the frequent bouts of plague, and so forth. By the sixth century the population had fallen dramatically, dwindling to a few thousand inhabitants. The once thriving urban fabric fell prey to "ruralization," as nature took over the vestiges of the ancient city.

In the seventh century the ancient city yielded to a desolate landscape of progressive decay and depopulation. At the same time the pagan lore was succumbing to a "Christianization" process. In the first decades of the fifteenth century, the developing Christian city was victoriously claimed by the papacy as its own, the City of the Popes. And

Mascaron water-spout from the wall-fountain in Via Giulia.

so, up until the Breach of Porta Pia on September 20, 1870, a city of indescribable beauty had gradually stratified over a span of some 450 years. In all this time the Tiber had served a central role, and for the papal city the abundant flow of water once more became one of its most characteristic features, as epitomized by the Trevi fountain.

In its later stages, under Pius IX, the papal city saw the steady regeneration of the population, and the renewal of its social and physical fabric. The growth initiated in the previous centuries underwent a dramatic boost, and after 1870 the city surged into a new era, with a new identity, becoming the Terza Roma or Third Rome, the newly founded capital of the Kingdom of Italy, and subsequently of the Italian Republic. But it was in this very transition to being a capital that Rome became "divorced" from its river.

Throughout its demographic and physical fluctuations Rome had always preserved an intimate link with the Tiber and the many other watercourses in its environs. But each of the three cities of Rome has its own characteristics, its own methods of production, institutions, government, religion, and not least its own ethnic, anthropological, and cultural composition. The uses of water have differed greatly from age to age, according to the diverse life styles, first of the ancient imperial and republican city, then of the Christian city and that of the popes, and finally of today's Rome, the last of the three cities.

The very difference in needs between the ancient capital and the ensuing Christian city are the reason for the demand for a more substantial water supply, and also for the collapse of the once superb system constructed in antiquity. The intensive renewal and rebuilding of the city's waterworks during papal rule was a response to the surge in the population, but it also enabled the pontiffs to highlight the supremacy of a city they had assumed as their own. Later, the dramatic demographic rise in the post-papal period necessitated urgent improvements to the system and a substantial increase to its delivery capacity, to meet modern-day demands.

The charming Botticella wall-fountain in Via di Ripetta (detail).

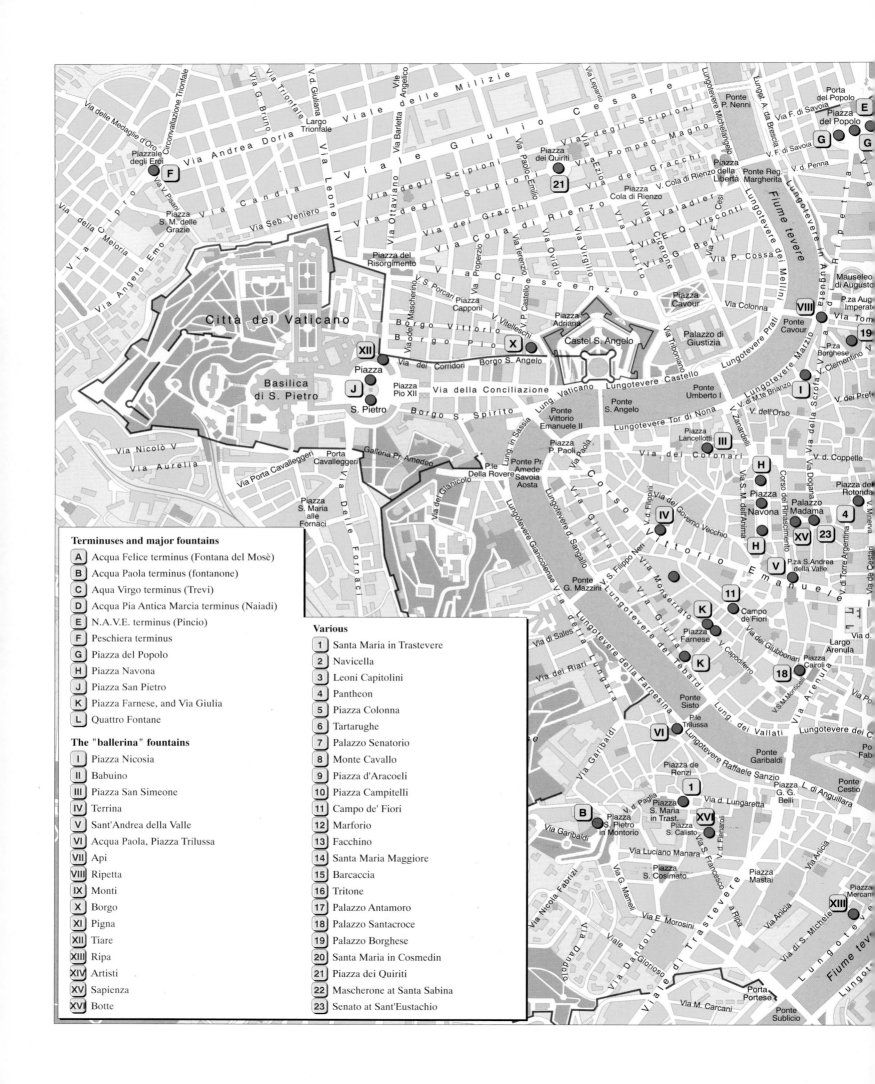

Terminuses and major fountains

- **A** Acqua Felice terminus (Fontana del Mosè)
- **B** Acqua Paola terminus (fontanone)
- **C** Aqua Virgo terminus (Trevi)
- **D** Acqua Pia Antica Marcia terminus (Naiadi)
- **E** N.A.V.E. terminus (Pincio)
- **F** Peschiera terminus
- **G** Piazza del Popolo
- **H** Piazza Navona
- **J** Piazza San Pietro
- **K** Piazza Farnese, and Via Giulia
- **L** Quattro Fontane

The "ballerina" fountains

- **I** Piazza Nicosia
- **II** Babuino
- **III** Piazza San Simeone
- **IV** Terrina
- **V** Sant'Andrea della Valle
- **VI** Acqua Paola, Piazza Trilussa
- **VII** Api
- **VIII** Ripetta
- **IX** Monti
- **X** Borgo
- **XI** Pigna
- **XII** Tiare
- **XIII** Ripa
- **XIV** Artisti
- **XV** Sapienza
- **XVI** Botte

Various

- **1** Santa Maria in Trastevere
- **2** Navicella
- **3** Leoni Capitolini
- **4** Pantheon
- **5** Piazza Colonna
- **6** Tartarughe
- **7** Palazzo Senatorio
- **8** Monte Cavallo
- **9** Piazza d'Aracoeli
- **10** Piazza Campitelli
- **11** Campo de' Fiori
- **12** Marforio
- **13** Facchino
- **14** Santa Maria Maggiore
- **15** Barcaccia
- **16** Tritone
- **17** Palazzo Antamoro
- **18** Palazzo Santacroce
- **19** Palazzo Borghese
- **20** Santa Maria in Cosmedin
- **21** Piazza dei Quiriti
- **22** Mascherone at Santa Sabina
- **23** Senato at Sant'Eustachio

ANCIENT ROME
(14TH CENT. B.C. TO 6TH CENT. A.D.)

A deep and indelible relationship binds Rome with its waters. The city itself was born from water. Before Romulus established his *Roma quadrata*, the archaic settlements on the slopes of the Roman hills had begun as riverside encampments. At that time the Tiber's banks washed the foot of the Palatine and Capitoline hills. But there were also numerous brooks and streams (including the Almonis and the *amnis Petronia*), together with freshwater springs (the Lupercal on the Palatine, the Juturna in the Forum, etc.), marshes (the Velabro Maggiore between the Aventine and Caelian hills, the Velabro Minore between the Viminal and Quirinal hills, the *Caprea* in the Campus Martius, etc.). Furthermore, in the city's environs and even within the urban fabric, a great number of wells drew on underground springs (some sulfurous or warm, others with specific mineral content, including the so-called Acqua Acetose and the Acque Albule).

The sheer abundance of the primal element of life explains why the writers of antiquity assigned the city the name of *Regina Aquarum*.

Early in the city's history, when the political focus of the city descended to the hollow between the Capitoline and Palatine hills, the time had come to harness the water brought by rain, to channel the effluent, and drain the stagnant pools of the nearby swamplands. The abundance of water on all sides called for a diligent program for regulating and canalizing this essential resource.

The decision to pave the Forum – in the spot where the fabled basket containing the twins Romulus and Remus had come to rest – necessitated a proper drainage scheme for the valley, which was all too often flooded by the Tiber's spates. Tradition credits the monarchies of the Etruscan dynasty with the first land reclamation scheme and the construction of a working drainage system, complete with a network of sewers and conduits (both open and underground), whose main feature was the Cloaca Maxima, a drain that channeled off the excess water – except in case of extensive inundation or flash floods – directly into the Tiber, passing through the Velabrum and the Forum Boarium.

The fordable point of the river, just below Tiber Island, soon became the site of a busy human crossroads that developed into a thriving hub of commercial exchange, where the principal trade causeways converged with the drover paths and cattle-tracks both to and from the sea, from the Etruscan north to Magna Graecia in the south of the peninsula and vice versa, from the Tyrrhenian coast to the interior, and back.

The hillsides around this river crossing, some of which rise to a height of 60–70 meters above sea level, granted an excellent environment for the burgeoning human settlements. The geography of the place afforded adequate defense, with slopes and the surrounding mires and marshes fed by rainwater and river spates. There were also potable freshwater springs and brooks in abundance.

Below the hills, near the ford itself and along the riverbanks, the terrain offered an ideal marketplace for the growing barter and trade activities. A natural emporium soon materialized, rapidly establishing itself as the fulcrum of local, interregional, and even Mediterranean trade, with a steady flow of merchants and tradespeople of all races and creeds, bringing goods of every possible kind.

Decorative architectural feature in the Villa Medici gardens.

Opposite
Bernini's fountain of the Bees, with its controversial dedication.

The reason for the site's particular success as a trading station is perhaps difficult for the modern observer to perceive, as Rome has long since been divorced from its river: the river and the economic activity of the city's population no longer enjoy the close relationship and symbiosis that characterized the simple first encampments B.C. up until the mid-1800s. Nonetheless, for some twenty-seven centuries Rome's function as a fluvial emporium was a fundamental part of its urban history.

Beside the Latini and Sabines, the river port attracted flocks of Italics, Etruscans, Greeks, and Phoenicians, thereby fostering the encounter and cross-fertilization of different cultures and civilizations. It nurtured the exchange of goods and ideas, and furthered a general permeability of religious and artistic influences, encouraging a tendency toward syncretism and multiethnic coexistence.

The Romans possessed a rare receptiveness toward the deities of other peoples, toward foreign cults, myths, and rites. The result of this openness was a growing syncretic pantheon, in which the gods of defeated populations were incorporated and readily worshiped. And while, in time, this pantheon was extended to include the Greek and Hellenistic world and the rest of the Orient, the original core of Roman culture remained Italo-Etruscan. The Etruscan cosmology included a great many aquatic divinities, by which springs and brooks were venerated as the founding generators of the Earth itself.

Foremost in the Etruscan pantheon was the Tiber, called *Pater Tiberinus*, the "Tiberine Father," who became the very symbol of the city and was celebrated each year on December 8 with a festival known as the *Tiberinalia*. Rome without the Tiber snaking through it is inconceivable, and often the river is pictured together with the twins Romulus and Remus, as if to underline the close ties between the city, its founder, and its river.

Other divinities of note are the nymphs or water-goddesses, who fulfilled crucial roles in traditional legend regarding the city's origins: the Nymph Egeria became the guide of one of Rome's earliest kings, Numa Pompilius, upon whose death the nymph wept so much she became a spring; the Nymph Carmentis, tutelary deity of the eponymous freshwater spring at the foot of the Palatine hill, became the goddess of childbirth and was honored by Rome's mothers in the *Carmentalia*, lasting January 11 to 15; the Nymph Juturna (or Diuturna), who has her spring in the Roman Forum, married Janus and gave birth to Fons, Fontus, and Fontanus, whose festival, celebrated on October 13, bears the name *Fontinalia*. On October 13 the early Romans would deck the fountains and springs with flowers to keep the god appeased, as without water there can be no life. To the god Fons they devoted an altar at the foot of the Janiculum, a temple, and even one of the city gates in the Walls of Servius, the Porta Fontinalis, which gave onto the Campus Martius and the Tiber.

Moreover, the sacred link between water and the pantheon of the traditional Etrusco-Roman religion was based on the element's irreplaceable role in the everyday life in the city. It was also a godsend for combating its opposite element, fire, which periodically devoured entire districts of the city.

As time wore on, the original village-like settlements merged to form an ever-growing urban mass, eventually becoming the city *par excellence*, the center of the entire *orbe* or known world (whence the motto *urbi et orbi*, to the city and the world). Rome also became the largest market of general consumption in antiquity.

For centuries the Tiber provided a vast navigable corridor serving the region, enabling the penetration of vessels to the heart of the city and thence to the interior of the peninsula. For centuries the banks of the Tiber hosted quays, wharves, and full-fledged river ports equipped with all the facilities necessary to supply a constantly growing capital: the Porto Tiberino Antico and the Porto Tiberino Nuovo at Testaccio; the ancient *Navalia* with the military arsenal upstream from Tiber Island; the link with the Tyrrhenian seaside town of Ostia, and with the ports built by Claudius and Trajan. These facilities mark the various phases of development of a vast self-replenishing port and the Tiber assumed the function of a *via maestra* for the constant restocking of this limitless market, into which flooded merchandise from all over the Mediterranean basin.

The fountain at the crossroads of Via Bissolati and Via San Basilio.

From time immemorial, the Tiber had offered a junction between the Via Campana on its right bank, toward the sea, and Via Salaria on its left, toward the interior. This

crossroads facilitated the trade of salt, a vital ingredient in the diet of men and their flocks. And although the number of herdsmen and livestock breeders had dwindled compared to the town's earlier days, the Romans continued their herding for centuries.

Though both god and "father," on occasion the Tiber suddenly turned against the city and burst its banks, flooding the surrounding land far and wide. The poorer quarters of the city were always the worst hit when the river was in spate, and consequently even the poorer neighborhoods inhabited by the *plebs* (Suburra and the Aventine) began to creep upward to escape the river's wrath.

Under the monarchies and during the first centuries of republican Rome the population possessed a sufficient water supply in the city's abundant natural springs. The river water itself was drinkable, and wells and cisterns were constantly replenished by rainfall. But as the town swelled its borders and the population grew, the problem of a constant and sufficient water supply became increasingly critical. The solution was to construct an aqueduct, a scheme by which fresh water might be conveyed from the outlying springs and brooks along manmade conduits, either raised or underground. Aqueducts are justly regarded as one of the Romans' most distinctive contributions to architecture, symbolizing their engineering skills. Some of these works concluded their itinerary with a *castellum aquae* or terminus, serving to redistribute the water to the various districts of the city. Such terminuses were designed to show off the water, sometimes as a monumental landmark and sometime as a *nymphaeum*.

The organized supply of water to the citizenry reinforced the juridical notion that water was a common good and part of the public domain. Only the state itself could dispense water for private use in the home, and the bestowal of a concession to use water – either to an individual or to a hereditary line – was the reserve of the city's rulers. A private supply of water for domestic use was a great privilege, and denoted rank and class. In the often ramshackle urban *insulae* or apartment blocks, the upper levels were the realm of the poor, and water was supplied to the ground story only. Otherwise it had to be fetched from the nearest public fountain.

Between 312 B.C. and A.D. 226 a total of eleven aqueducts (some with subsidiary branches) were built and successively upkept, enlarged, and improved upon over the years. While the major Claudia and Anio Novus aqueducts fed all Rome's outlying regions, each district was served by at least three or four hydraulic subsystems of its own.

The aqueducts of Rome, including the Aqua Appia and the Aqua Alexandriana, provided an important model for the provinces of the Roman empire, near and far, and the capital's engineers were universally acknowledged for their masterful exploitation of the natural water supply. The writers of antiquity (particularly the Greeks) noted that the Romans' cultural superiority was exemplified by their construction of roads, aqueducts, and drains. A rough though credible estimate of the overall volume of water channeled by the Roman water system in the third century B.C. amounts to a million cubic meters per day. In 1980 that figure was 1,815,000 cubic meters, providing a supply of 13,000 liters per second.

Visitors to Rome in the days of Emperor Augustus marveled at the sheer abundance of water throughout the city, which boasted around 700 watering basins, 500 public fountains, and 130 service reservoirs. The prodigal supply of fresh water to Rome meant that there was plenty not only for private domestic use and public amenities (the public baths, for instance), but also for purely aesthetic applications such as architectural terminuses and artistic fountains. Unlike the more utilitarian uses of water, such as the pools and tubs for public use, Rome's fountains were often purely decorative and earned the city great fame, together with the spectacular *nymphaea* mentioned above. Among the early city's many water displays was the *Meta Sudans*, a towering cone of porous rock oozing water which once stood close by the Arch of Constantine in the grounds of the Colosseum, marking the junction of four or five of the Fourteen Regions of the city in the time of Augustus. Another important landmark was the *Septizonium*, built under Septimius Severus on the southern corner of the Palatine to create a spectacular approach to the imperial *palatia* for those entering Rome from the Porta Appia or the Porta Latina.

One of the massive twin fountains in Saint Peter's Square.

The somewhat weathered bas-relief of a sow, which gave Via della Scrofa its name; in 1870 the fountain was dismantled and its basin reused elsewhere.

Fountain in the courtyard of the Seminary in Via della Scrofa.

The Facchino or Water-carrier fountain in Via Lata.

Among the many public entertainments held in early Rome were the mock sea fights. These were grandiose public entertainments in which slaves and gladiators (or prisoners of war) engaged in fierce combat, usually to the death. This particular type of spectacle took place in a flooded arena inside a purpose-built theater, known as a *naumachia*. Attempts were made to equip the Colosseum for staging sea-battles, but this practice was quickly interrupted owing to the difficulty of containing the enormous volume of water required for the event. It had already been a terrific feat of engineering to construct the building on the site of Nero's *stagnum domus aureae*, a small lake attached to the fabled Golden House. At any event, three *naumachiae* are recorded in Rome: Caesar's in the Campus Martius, Augustus' in Trastevere, and Domitian's on the Vatican hill.

Without doubt, the most widespread public use of water in imperial times was in the thermal baths. Like the aqueducts, the Roman *thermae* embody not only the architecture of ancient Rome but also the city's culture and civilization, epitomizing the very lifestyle of the Romans, which was principally a socializing, urban lifestyle.

Not only in the capital, but in the entire orbit of the Romanized world, the construction of aqueducts, rainwater drains, thermal baths, and latrines was considered as essential as the construction of the streets and the various defensive works. In Roman cities throughout the empire, water and hygiene went hand in hand, and were considered indispensable features of the society's daily social order. The safeguarding of public hygiene naturally involved ensuring that both communal and private latrines were served by a ready supply of water, preferably flowing.

Dating from the times of Octavian's admiral Agrippa (63–12 B.C.), the grand imperial thermal baths were built for the purpose of public enjoyment and to encourage hygiene among the populace. At the same time, these gathering places performed a key role in the social and political development of the city. Together with *panem et circenses* (i.e., food and entertainment), the spas were seen as a means of maintaining public order. The notion of personal cleanliness stemmed from the custom of thermal baths, which in turn came to reflect the culture of *mens sana in corpore sano*.

The baths were the daily refuge of the unemployed, a place for idling away one's time, and at the same time a retreat from the poor sanitary conditions in the home, which was typically without a toilet or other facilities. Housing was often merely somewhere to retire to for the night, a place to collect one's daily *sportula* or allowance distributed by one's patron, or to receive the *frumentationes* and other public hand-outs, which were a kind of gratuity disbursed to the *plebs* in exchange for its vote. Needless to say, a free supply of water formed part of this allowance.

The frequent invasions of the Germanic hordes from the North grimly revealed the military shortcomings of the late Empire, and in A.D. 275–277 Aurelian began to fortify the city by constructing the first imposing defensive wall. Almost five centuries later the Empire faced new aggressions and sieges. Even today the walls are still called after Aurelian, despite their having been reworked, restored, and buttressed in the ensuing centuries (principally by Maxentius, Honorius, Belisarius). Not long after their construction, the question was raised about guaranteeing a proper supply of water within the walls. In the specific case of where today's Porta Maggiore stands, the gateway to the city coincides with the triple duct from three separate sources (Marcia, Tepula, and Julia) running alongside the channel for the Aqua Claudia and the Anio Novus.

At the beginning of the fourth century A.D. Rome boasted the world's most complex and best-articulated system of water supply and distribution, which was equipped with pumping stations for raising water, where necessary, toward the higher levels of the city. This system furnished water to the *domus* or single-family dwelling, to the ground story of the *insula* or more humble apartment block, and likewise to the monumental bath houses, and a total of 856 public baths, 15 *nymphaea*, 5 *naumachiae*, and 1,352 sundry pools and fountains dotted about the city. In this same period the Romans faced their first water crisis during the time of Galerius' siege, in A.D. 307.

The fourth century A.D. saw the end of the Western Empire, and although Rome lost its title as capital it remained a vital religious hub and a doubly sacred city: it was the

One of the sea-god water-spouts from the Neptune fountain in Piazza Navona, complete with crabs and water-baby.

home both of the traditional Roman cults and of the new persuasion of Christianity. The great landowners continued to endow the city with monuments and ensure the proper functioning of its facilities. They also hoped to control the traditional Roman religion, which the Christians disparagingly defined as pagan. The Christian emperor Constantine was forced to build the new creed's basilicas away from the city center, and even outside the city walls, respecting the ancient religious and political core of Rome. Not to be defeated, he founded Constantinople (modern Istanbul), making it the new capital of Christendom. The traditionalist elite lost their struggle for supremacy at the close of the century, however, when the Roman aristocracy itself began to defect to the Christian religion, and power shifted from the upper echelons of the late imperial setup to the hierarchs of the new Church.

Meanwhile, water continued to command an important position in all religion. Throughout Christian hagiography the sacred bond between water and religious activity is constant. Water is present in the two miracles performed by Peter (the leader of the Apostles), and Paul (the apostle of the Gentiles): the former causes water to gush forth from rock in the *tullianum* or underground execution cell of the prison at Rome, enabling him to perform the baptismal rites on two fellow prisoners, Processus and Martinianus; whereas Paul, a *bona fide* citizen of the capital, was beheaded (whereas Peter the Jew was crucified), and from the spot where his head fell, three springs gushed forth, whence the site's name of Tre Fontane.

In the fifth century the city walls were unable to stem the invasion of the Visigoths under their leader Alaric (A.D. 410), nor keep out the hordes of Vandals led by the gifted chieftain Gaiseric in A.D. 455. But the senatorial and landowning aristocracy continued to furnish the city with supplies and meet its principal needs, standing in for the absent emperor. While Rome was no longer the effective capital of the Empire, the abundance of water remained one of its prime characteristics. The popularity of the thermal baths was waning, due to the new impositions of the Christian faith regarding the human body, which were prompted not so much by an aversion to sexual matters, as by a growing squeamishness regarding bodily functions in general and a disinclination for collective bathing. Toward the close of the century Rome was overrun by the troops of the German warrior Odoacer (A.D. 476), but soon after, the occupying Ostragoth leader Theodoric furthered restoration work on the beleaguered city, including enhancements to its system of aqueducts.

In the fourth century Rome relinquished its claim to the title of *Regina Aquarum* or Queen of the Waters. The protracted hardships of the Byzantine-Gothic war (A.D. 535–553), together with plagues and repeated famines, precipitated the desertification of the peninsula. The city of Rome was depopulated, and each time it was besieged its aqueducts were a conspicuously convenient target. During his onslaught in 537 King Witigis of the Goths destroyed a great many stretches of the aqueducts so as to cut off the city's water supply. Shortly after, the general of the Byzantine troops, Belisarius, bricked up the archways of the remaining stretches of raised conduits so as to prevent invaders from penetrating the city.

The event heralded a new phenomenon (which would be repeated in the coming years until 1870). The manumission of the Aqua Traiana effectively cut the power supply to the mills ranged along the aqueduct's route on the slopes of the Janiculum. In order to cope with the demand for flour, new mills were immediately built on the Tiber both upstream and downstream from Tiber Island, taking advantage of the force of the river's steady flow. This notwithstanding, the Byzantine commander Belisarius was determined to restore Trajan's aqueduct to working order for the Janiculum flour mills.

After the war, during the ephemeral reconquest of the Italian peninsula, Rome was sorely neglected. The population was in rapid decline. The restoration of the surviving aqueducts would have required vast investments and only the Traiana, Marcia, Claudia, Alexandriana, and Virgo waters actually reached the city.

The bishop of Rome had by this time acquired considerable prestige throughout Christendom by setting his city above the major oriental metropolises – Alexandria,

A rugged river-god from the Fiumi or Rivers fountain in Piazza Navona.

Antioch, and Constantinople – gradually acquiring supremacy in the West. It is significant that the papal role goes by the name of *pontifex*, or "builder of bridges." The bishop of Rome was heir to the highest station of priesthood of the city's traditional religion, and therefore heir to the institutional duty to construct and make good the bridges over the Tiber, thereby reinforcing the sacred link with water.

The influence of the pope and of the clergy had rapidly become fundamental to the city's survival. Only the Church of Rome, with its unbounded properties, was in a position to furnish the primary necessities, such as foodstuffs and an adequate supply of water, weaponry, and soldiers.

At the close of the sixth century the pontificate of Gregory I ushered in the definitive eclipse of the ancient city and the dawn of the new Christian capital. In the year 602 Pope Gregory observed that the aqueducts were nearing collapse, despite the hasty repair work that had been carried out.

View of the nymphaeum at Villa Aldobrandini in Magnanapoli.

A COMMON MISPERCEPTION

It is worth taking a closer look at the accepted account of the barbarian rampages that are reputed to have hastened the demise of the aqueducts. The orthodox version has enabled historians to conveniently avoid examining the facts in greater detail.

In the fourth century the main water system built in antiquity had ceased to function, together with its eleven aqueducts and numerous branch conduits. At the same time, there was no longer any call for the great public water displays that had earned Rome the title of *Regina Aquarum*.

In the early Middle Ages Rome's water supply consisted of a reduced system of four or five aqueducts, which conveyed a meager current of fresh water to the various inhabited pockets of the old city. The Aqua Traiana fed the Trastevere ward and the Vatican; the Aqua Claudia and Aqua Alexandriana (the latter with various branches from other aqueducts) served the southern district of the city, as far as Ripa; the Aqua Virgo carried water to the neighborhood in the curve as far as Trastevere. As for Rome's rulers, the great medieval popes are all lauded for their efforts to restore the city's water supply.

The final blow to this impoverished water system was not, as it is generally claimed, delivered by the Goths but by major calamities of a natural order, namely, the numerous terrific floods (589, 717, 791, 1150, 1230, and so on), and the earthquakes (394, 557, 801, 1348, etc.). Add to this a succession of devastating wars and the steady disappearance of the technological skills (including that of the impoundment of spring water) for which Roman engineering was famous. And yet, in the later Middle Ages the Aqua Virgo, and perhaps the Aqua Alexandriana, continued to channel its waters, albeit sparse, into the Christian city, perhaps because for most of their course the conduits ran underground.

Opposite
Detail of the Moor fountain in Piazza Navona, and a view of the Barcaccia fountain at the foot of the Spanish Steps.

CHRISTIAN ROME
(7TH TO EARLY 15TH CENT.)

In 609, with the consent of Phocas, the ruling emperor, the pontiff Boniface IV transformed the Pantheon (the seat of all the divinities of the traditional Roman religions) into the Christian church of Santa Maria ad Martyres. The consecration of the Pantheon marked the ultimate demise of the ancient city, and heralded a program by which the new church committed itself to completing the Christianization of Rome, a pledge made initially by Constantine the Great. The Christian symbol of the cross appeared atop each place of worship, and church bells rang out in proclamation of the pope's physical and temporal dominion over the city.

The disastrous invasions of the previous century had brought utter abandon to the fabric of many areas of the city, from the Aventine and Esquiline to the Campus Martius and the Pincio. The surviving population huddled in a few select areas, particularly in the bight of the river, in Trastevere, and around the large basilicas of the Vatican, the Lateran, and Ostia.

Though still standing, the once busy bath houses languished in a state of sorry abandon. The widespread urban decay and the depleted population (in a thousand years the number of inhabitants had withered to below 100,000, with low points of a few tens of thousands) is confirmed by the scant demand for fresh water. The pontiffs restored those aqueducts that admitted quick repair (Traiana, Marcia, Claudia, Alexandriana, and Virgo). The yield of the aqueducts was minimal, but renovation on a larger scale was out of the question. Consequently, the inhabitants tended to occupy the lower areas, which were supplied by underground conduits.

In the seventh century the banks of the Tiber witnessed a series of military enhancements. The steady advance of the northern Lombards was progressively hemming in and isolating the various Byzantine dominions. For the Roman "duchy" the communications via river and sea were their only means for ensuring the replenishment of vital supplies and military aid.

The *Ripa Graeca* on the left bank of the Tiber became home to a flourishing colony of Byzantine seamen, merchants, soldiers, prostitutes, and saint-worshipers, all from the provinces of the East. Meanwhile, the *Ripa Romea* on the right bank saw the materialization of a new service specializing in repairing and replenishing the ships of religious pilgrims (the "Romei"), who had journeyed from afar to witness for themselves the New Jerusalem, the newfound holy city of western Christendom. These pious wayfarers were particularly keen to visit the tombs of the Christian martyrs, not least that of Saint Peter himself, on which the Church of Rome's very claim to supremacy was based.

The mounting needs of the pilgrims forced the pope and clergy to shore up the Aqua Traiana and carry out improvements to the Vatican area. While the slopes of the Janiculum offered a serviceable site for bodily evacuation (and earned the indecorous name of *Mons Cacatorius*, meaning Defecation Hill), near the Vatican basilica it became imperative to set up proper latrines, fitted out with washing facilities and running water. Once renovated, the aqueduct's delivery capacity also made it possible to run water straight to the fountain in the so-called "Paradise" or atrium of the basilica, a feature that the Romei or pilgrims were to duly record as one of the marvels of their host city.

Detail from the fountain at Palazzo Santacroce.

Opposite
One of the rearing horses from the Rivers fountain in Piazza Navona.

Through until the eighth century the waters of the Aqua Marcia continued to flow into the city, albeit at a reduced rate. Thereafter, Pope Adrian I (r. 772–795) was obliged to effect extensive repairs to the Aquae Traiana and Claudia (serving the Lateran via Nero's branch to the Caelian and the Palatine), together with the Aqua Marcia, and particularly the Aqua Virgo.

Over the years, repairs were also made to the aqueducts that had survived the disasters of the sixth century. The delivery capacity was steadily diminishing, however, and as the centuries wore on, water only arrived in the public basins and a handful of ecclesiastical properties. In the late eighth and early ninth centuries the Aquae Claudia and Virgo were consolidated. Pope Gregory IV (r. 827–844) ordered further repairs to the aqueduct built by Trajan (which had been known as the Sabatino aqueduct since the days of Emperor Hadrian), but at the end of the ninth century the Aqua Traiana disappeared, together with the mills on the slopes of the Janiculum.

The economic stasis that gripped Rome during these centuries had turned the city into a wilderness of non-productivity. The abandonment of the farmland went hand in hand with the steady turning into marshland of the *ager Romanus* and *ager Pontinus*. The spates and flooding were now aggravated by another form of water-induced destruction.

The Tiber continued to be a vital channel for replenishment and supply, as the ports along its banks provided a constant link with the open sea routes. The once generous fund of slave labor was no more, but the river offered an indefatigable source of energy to power the growing number of flour mills, the textile works, the water-driven hammers of the ironsmiths, the windlasses of the leatherworkers and manufacturers of cordage and rigging.

The ninth century saw the conversion to new uses of many of the large buildings that had served the societies of antiquity. Although they had long been shorn of their precious metal fittings and their embellishments in marble (the statues and other pieces of marble unceremoniously disappeared into the limekilns of the *calcararii* to make mortar for new constructions), these buildings nonetheless still boasted their lofty vaulted ceilings and massive concrete pillars. Among the best-conserved edifices of ancient Rome were those fortunate enough to be converted to religious or civic uses as churches, ecclesiastical facilities, municipal warehouses, *xenodochia* or hospices, and so forth. The once grandiloquent thermal bathhouses were left to molder and collapse, however, as the ancient Roman culture of socializing around the practice of communal bathing had fallen into disuse.

The new Christian city had no place for either spas or water spectacles. The life-giving fluid was available only from the utility fountains or public tubs. Centuries of economic blight and urban decay had depleted the Romans' technical skills in organizing and guaranteeing an extensive water system throughout the city. Even the term *aquaeductus* lost currency in favor of the word *forma*.

The few aqueducts that had survived the administrative collapse of the Roman state and the waves of invasion and siege (not to mention the natural calamities) were in a dismal state and barely fulfilled their function. At this stage in the city's history, use was revived of the Traiana, Alexandriana, and Virgo aqueducts, as they largely ran underground and were the best conserved. But the discharge rate was poor and the water itself often unfit for consumption, partly because of the lack of maintenance on the conduits at the source, and partly because of the general decrepitude of the entire system.

After the year 1000 the city's inhabitants continued to cluster about the bight of the river, between Ponte Sant'Angelo and Ponte Senatorio or Santa Maria (what used to be Ponte Sant'Emilio was renamed Ponte Rotto – i.e., broken – after it collapsed in the terrible flood of 1598). Now the city's main source of potable water was the river itself. Not surprisingly, among the *arti romane* or guilds, the ones representing the *acquaroli* or *acquarenari* increased in importance: they were the builders of the *aquaricae*, the large clay receptacles used for transporting and decanting the river water.

From the eleventh to thirteenth centuries, like many other cities, Rome enjoyed a durable phase of rejuvenation and growth that witnessed a rise in the population, an expanding economy, extensive building, and political change. The population, however, was still living in scattered pockets of fabric. Stranded in a morass of ruin and decay,

Opposite
The ancient kantharos from the fountain at Santa Cecilia in Trastevere.

Following pages
View of the Cupid fountain at Villa Doria Pamphilj.

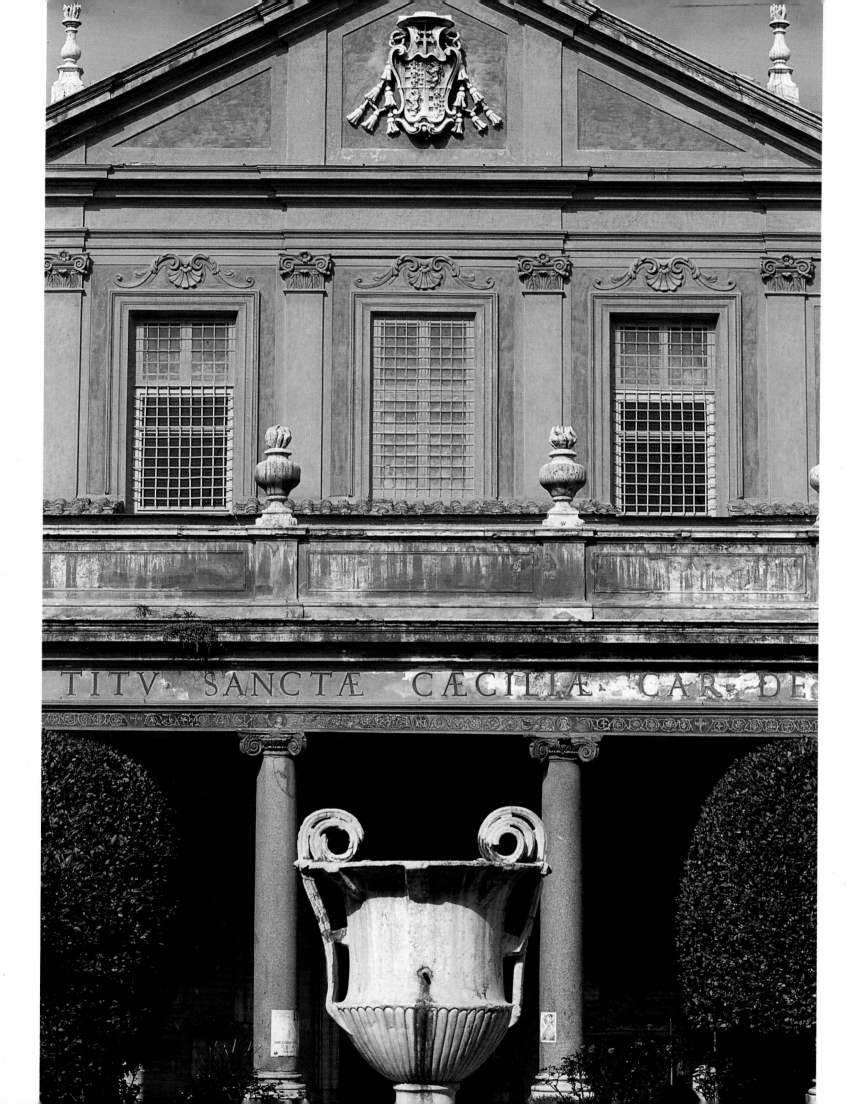

these islands of habitation were nonetheless still girdled by the Aurelianic walls, which now hung loosely round a shrunken *urbs*. Three of these islands – the bight, Trastevere, and Borgo – were close enough to the Tiber's banks to make the retrieval of river water an easy matter.

Rather than lay on channeled water according to need, it had become simpler to locate industrial facilities near the water's edge (mills, cloth factories, and ironworks), together with the host of small crafts outfits (tanners, dyers, butchers, and so forth), which required running water to clear off the foul-smelling wastes involved in production. There was one exception, however. In order to render serviceable the Aqua Claudia (which carried water to the Lateran and its environs), in 1122 Pope Callixtus II (r. 1119–24) had a new open channel built that redirected water from the Aquae Julia and Tepula into an underground duct leading to the Claudian aqueduct; from here the water reemerged outside Porta Furba as far as Porta Metronia, after which it reached the Circus Maximus, Santa Maria in Cosmedin, and thenceforth the Tiber.

This channel, known variously as the *marrana* or *marana* (a term which has since come to mean any small open water duct) was the property of the basilica of San Giovanni, and was built to irrigate the fields in addition to supplying hydraulic power to the plethora of small activities scattered through the southern sector of the city (which remained scantily populated until around 1870). Through a piece of verbal sleight-of-hand, from the fifteenth century onward this *marana* (and its sibling, the *maranella*), known also as the Aqua Crabra, acquired an "i" and the rather improbable title of "Aqua Mariana."

According to a document dated August 10, 1204, the arches of a substantial stretch of the raised aqueduct of Nero's branch conduit from the Aqua Claudia were walled up, as they no longer actually carried water. The handsome brick construction was incorporated into the fortifications for the Lateran patriarchate. Alas, during one of the many struggles between factions, the aqueduct was eventually destroyed altogether.

By the dawn of the fourteenth century Rome's population had grown apace with its buoyant economic activities. The city had also acquired political and administrative independence from the papacy, but not without a penalty. The sudden transfer to Avignon in France of the pontiff and the Curia (with its retinue of lawyers and magistrates, brokers and bankers, artists and craftsmen, literati and militia, *avventurieri* and prostitutes, ecclesiastics and wheeler-dealers) harbingered an enduring term of urban decline. The steady disgregation of the blighted urban fabric was hastened in mid-century by a new bout of plague and uprisings. The number of inhabitants fell to the low levels recorded in the sixth century, and the problems of proper water supply paled beside those of everyday survival during the interminable wars raging both inside and outside the city. The statutes of 1363 state categorically that the Curia Capitolina was under obligation to safeguard the Aqua Virgo and upkeep its conduits, *and* to forestall private abuse of the supply. In the meanwhile, the flow had shrunk to a trickle, as the springs at Salone Vecchio (near Tivoli) were no longer connected to the Aqua Virgo system, which had therefore to rely solely on the discharge from the Bocca di Leone in Via Tiburtina.

When the papacy and its entourage resettled in Rome the hoped-for benefits to the city were not forthcoming, as almost immediately the Great Schism with the West broke out. The rupture was so great that the relative autonomy thitherto enjoyed by the town council was abrogated, and the papacy symbolically took up position in Adrian's former mausoleum, which controlled the Tiber at Ponte Sant'Angelo and hence the transit of people in the high-density area of the so-called Città Leonina.

The main source of drinking-water was now the river, whose waters were carefully stored in vats in cellars and cooled with snow (in underground ice-houses). River water was even preferred to the remaining supply issued by the aqueducts, or indeed to the fresh water from the Janiculum springs.

In the years that followed, all that remained of the city's once glorious water-supply system disappeared with the physical collapse of the last aqueducts. Those that continued to work, albeit haltingly, were the underground conduits of the Aqua Virgo, and perhaps those of the Aqua Alexandriana.

The nymphaeum at Palazzo Borghese, known as the "Bath of Venus."

PIVS IIII
PONTIFEX
MAXIMVS

PIVS IIII
PONTIFEX
MAXIMVS

Papal Rome
(EARLY 15TH CENT. TO 1870)

In the first half of the fifteenth century the problem of an efficient water supply lurched once again to the foreground. With the definitive return of the papacy in the person of the Colonna pope, Martin V (r. 1417–31), the Christian City was rapidly transfigured into the Papal City. One of the immediate effects of this change was a surge in the population, and with it, the demand for running water.

For the coming centuries, through until 1870, a chain of successive popes poured effort and commitment into improving and enlarging the city as the concrete expression of the papacy's absolute primacy and the universal supremacy of the Church of Rome.

The new Papal City was to be a symbol of stone and brick, and boasted an extensive system of waterworks. Indeed, water made a spectacular comeback in the context of a new architectural style, the baroque.

In the centuries that preceded the industrial age (and in fact the Papal State did not join the revolution until some way through the nineteenth century) the city maintained its close ties with its river. Up until the days of Pius IX, the Tiber continued to be a puissant commercial channel bearing cargoes to and from the sea and ferrying goods in and out of the inland provinces. The Tiber was the only lifeline for this center of fervent consumption, which was as if marooned in a wasteland of inertia and non-productivity. In response to demand, the wharves and docks along the river-front increased in size and number, such as Ripa Romea (later Ripa Grande), the so-called Ripetta, the Legnara alla Tinta, and the Travertini (later Porto Leonino). The Travertini docks played a particularly important role in transporting stone for the building of New Saint Peter's and subsequently Bernini's vast baroque colonnade encircling the square.

In time, both the Tiber and the city's wells and cisterns ensured a consistent supply of water for general use, especially in the low-lying quarters of the city. Like those who lived higher up, however, the papacy's swelling urban agglomerate was also penalized by the inadequate water pressure. With the advent of Nicholas V (r. 1447–55) the city's water supply returned to the top of the papal agenda, and attention was turned to resuscitating the ancient aqueducts and providing flowing water, at the very least for the public fountains.

In 1452 Pope Nicholas issued an ordinance prescribing the liabilities of the various *Magistri aedificiorum et stratarum*, including their obligations concerning the fountains and water supply "dentro et fora de mura" (both within and without the city walls). The members of this urban judiciary body were required to keep a vigil on the "de treyo" (Trevi) fountain and the conduits of the Aqua Virgo with monthly visits to monitor and repair breaches in the conduits and sewers. A commemorative slab of 1453 declaims the works sponsored by the pontiff Nicholas, who, after filling Rome with magnificent monuments to the Faith, personally ordered and disbursed sums for the restoration and enlargement of the fountain facing the Piazza dei Crociferi, trasnfigured in the eighteenth century into one of Rome's most celebrated sights, the world-famous Trevi fountain, thereby restoring it to its former glory. Furthermore, the pontiff transformed three small medieval basins into a single rectangular pool, set against a castelated wall

The Moses fountain, central arch and carved marble balustrade.

The Moses fountain (with detail).

The forbidding but rather ungainly central figure of the Moses fountain.

with three gushing spouts, facing east toward Via Lata (now Via del Corso); the successive eighteenth-century *mostra* or water-spectacle was installed toward the south.

The Vatican's involvement in the aqueduct and the *mostra* was undoubtedly spurred by Nicholas V, who appointed Nello di Bartolomeo da Bologna works supervisor. (By the way, there is no evidence to substantiate the claim that the design was by Leon Battista Alberti or by Bernardo Rossellino.)

At all events, the restoration of the fountain (together with the reinstatement of the bridges, roads, and other primary infrastructure), was part of a carefully pondered strategy: while Nicholas admittedly shouldered the expenses, in exchange he effectively arrogated to himself the functions technically due the civil magistracies, as if to underscore the fact that the pope carried a share in the city's renewal because Rome was fundamentally the City of the Popes. In truth, Nicholas' restoration work on the Aqua Virgo system was modest, but signaled the first shots of a program of papal administrative intervention applied in the course of the century to ensure a water supply that matched the constantly expanding city. The popes took an interest in the upkeep of the Aqua Virgo because it became increasingly important for the more densely populated quarter of the river bight and adjacent Campus Martius, the critical focuses of the papal city's expansion. This was the future site of the so-called baroque quarter, which would in the course of time engulf other neighboring wards.

Still in the second half of the fifteen century, in 1466–67 the Bourbon pope, Paul II (r. 1464–71), made further improvements to the Aqua Virgo, and soon after, Sixtus IV della Rovere inaugurated a program in preparation for the Holy Year of 1475, which included making good the vaulted archways of the raised aqueduct from the Pincio to the Trevi fountain.

In 1535, when Rome was still reeling from the rampages of the Lanzichenecchi or German mercenaries, Pope Paul III (r. 1534–49) undertook to restore the springs of Salone Vecchio, near Tivoli, to increase the capacity of the Aqua Virgo. The improvement scheme was followed up by his successor Pius IV (r. 1559–65), a member of the Medici family, who prodded the lethargic Camera Capitolina into activity. Despite his efforts, the project remained unfinished. The effective rehabilitation of the old freshwater springs and the renovation of the conduits only came with the reign of the Ghislieri pope, Pius V (r. 1566–72), who presided at the formal opening of the newly restored aqueduct on August 16, 1570. However, it soon became apparent that a more widespread, unifying scheme was needed for distributing water efficiently to the public fountains and watering places, together with adequate means for laying on running water to private homes – particularly to the residences of the nobility.

Later that year a committee of cardinals was appointed to oversee matters of water supply (whose members included Giovanni Ricci da Montepulciano, and Cardinal Ferdinando de' Medici, successive owners of the Villa Medici on the Pincio, which would draw abundantly on the service). The committee's first move was to contract the architect Giacomo Della Porta – who had already worked on restructuring the aqueduct – to build a large reservoir below the Pincio and a new hydraulic network boasting some five kilometers of piping to serve the wards of Campus Martius, Ponte, Parione, Sant'Eustachio, Pigna, Trevi, and Campitelli, among others. The cardinals also commissioned Della Porta to construct a further eighteen fountains to adorn the city.

This second project was continued under the pontificate of Gregory XIII (r. 1572–85) and his successor Sixtus V (r. 1585–90), though only half the proposed fountains were actually realized, namely those in Piazza del Popolo (1589), Piazza Colonna (1575), Piazza Navona (two, 1574), Campo de' Fiori (1581–90), Piazza del Pantheon (1579), Piazza San Marco (1588), Piazza Montanara (1589), and Piazza Giudìa (completed in 1591, after Sixtus' death).

Gregory XIII was remembered by his contemporaries as the "fountain pope," owing to his concerted efforts to provide the common townsfolk with their principal source of fresh water. He also midwifed a broad program devoted to improving the city's water reserves by initiating the restoration of the conduits of the Aqua Claudia, which had ceased to function in the Middle Ages. This project was indispensable for guaranteeing a regular supply to the hills in the east of the city, an important reserve of open land that served the programmed expansion of the ever-swelling papal city. The pope's building agenda gave a decisive boost to the urbanization of the hillsides through the construction of a vast grain repository, known locally as the Granarone, on the Quirinal near the Baths of Diocletian.

The next pope, Sixtus V, born Felice Perretti, inherited his predecessor's building program and in the space of two years the defunct sources of the Aqua Alexandriana were restored to working order. Furthermore, an additional twenty-two miles of new conduits were commissioned (both underground and raised, exploiting the existing arches of the Aquae Marcia and Claudia). Sixtus upstaged his predecessor, however, by renaming the ancient Aqua Alexandriana serving the Quirinal and the Esquiline after himself. The role of the new Acqua Felice system was basically to ensure proper supply to the papal residence and to the grounds, garden plots, and fountains of the Villa Montalto (no longer existing), which the pontiff had had built while still a cardinal.

THE FONTANA DEL MOSÈ

The fountain's design was first entrusted to Matteo Bartolani, whose miscalculation of the flow capacity of the conduits resulted in a meager and weak discharge in the square, with no hope of increasing the quota. To remedy matters the authorities called in the brother of the renowned engineer and architect Domenico Fontana, Giovanni, who proceeded to connect a further fifty-two smaller springs to the system, thereby boosting the effective outflow and final jet of water. In 1587 a "provisional" water display commemorating the Acqua Felice was therefore installed, but this was not really capable of supplying running water to the neighborhood until two years later, with the intervention of Domenico Fontana, working alongside the aforementioned Bartolani.

The *mostra terminale* of the new Acqua Felice at Santa Susanna (known as the Moses fountain) was styled after one of antiquity's most representative forms of architecture, the triumphal arch, which is exemplified by the triple *fornices* of the "Trophies of Marius," whose vestiges are still visible in today's Piazza Vittorio Emanuele II, basically all that remains of the *nymphaeum* built by Septimius Severus early in the third century on the Esquiline, perhaps drawing its supply from the Aqua Claudia or Anio Novus.

The *fornices* or arches of the Roman aqueduct were the fountain's inspiration, and Domenico drew liberally on the triple-arch-*nymphaeum* motif to celebrate his achievement of having successfully brought water to the city's eastern hillsides.

The provisional *mostra* soon became a permanent landmark and was enhanced with sculptures. Three large niches are set below a tall attic story, on which an escutcheon borne by angels surmounts an inscription commemorating Sixtus V's undertaking. The side niches are graced with bas-reliefs: on the left, *Joseph lets the Jews cross the dried-up Jordan River* (by Flaminio Vacca and Pier Paolo Olivieri), and on the right, *Aaron leads the Jews to drink* (Giovan Battista Della Porta). The central niche contains a colossal statue of Moses (by Leonardo Sormani and Prospero Bresciano, 1588), which was promptly derided for its inept proportions. From a spout at the base of each niche water gushes into basins adorned with four lions. These were not matching: two in gray porphyry had been brought from the Pantheon fountain, and the other two had once graced the side of the basilica of San Giovanni in Laterano; at any event, the originals were moved by Gregory XVI to the Musei Vaticani and replaced with copies. Lastly, the enclosure protecting the fountain was likewise recouped from a building erected in the time of Pius IV.

The general lack of proportion among the monument's elements is most likely due to the poor coordination of the various phases of construction. Initially, Domenico Fontana sketched out in rough the overall architecture of the monument, which was executed without bearing in mind the subsequent decoration. The pope then had him fill the niches, soliciting him to adorn the central one with a statue of Moses (perhaps prompted by Michelangelo's imposing *Moses* in Saint Peter's). The pontiff's wish was met and the bas-reliefs and central statue hastily executed, alas, with scant attention to proportion.

Perhaps the fountain's most unappealing feature is the disgruntled, even surly, look on the prophet's face. Furthermore, the envisaged vista of the original installation was impaired when the nineteenth-century Palazzo Amici di Gaetano Koch was demolished to make way for Via Barberini and Via Bissolati. Before the Quirinal-bound extension of Via XX Settembre was opened in the 1920s, this sixteenth-century fountain had an ample backdrop on either side.

One of the ornamental posts from the Fontanone of the Acqua Paola on the Janiculum.

The aqueduct was quickly extended from Santa Susanna to Monte Cavallo (Piazza del Quirinale), where it supplied the Quirinal fountain beneath the huge statues of the Dioscuri, Castor and Pollux, the patrons of horsemanship. Water became so crucial to the papal city that the canals and conduits of Via Pia (now Via XX Settembre) dictated the pavement level and the way the square itself was arranged. Subsequently, new clay pipes were laid – financed by the Camera Capitolina – to carry the Acqua Felice's water to the Forum and the Campidoglio or Capitol, where, after a lapse of some centuries, the fountains of Piazza Capitolina and Aracoeli once again flowed with water. Within a few years the Acqua Felice network was enlarged to supply not only the hills but also the lower districts of the city in the hollow below the Capitol. Two subsidiary pipelines were built to distribute water to other areas of the sprawling Monti ward: one departed from Porta Maggiore in the direction of the Lateran and the Caelian, the other from San Lorenzo, bound for the neighborhood of Santa Maria Maggiore.

Sixtus' successor Gregory XIV (1590–91) approved further enlargements to the network of the Acqua Felice, and in the space of a few years this "modern" aqueduct serviced a vast area comprising Trastevere, Borgo, and the hospital at Santo Spirito in Sassia.

This was only the first of a long sequence of improvements made to the Acqua Felice system (the last in 1870), making the aqueduct and its tributary network the mainstay of the city's water distribution.

Shortly after his election the Borghese pope, Paul V (r. 1605–21), undertook the repair of the Aqua Traiana (mistakenly presumed to be the imperial Aqua Alsietina), to meet the demand for water in Trastevere, Borgo and the Vatican enclave itself on the right bank of the Tiber. The supply was also extended to the various left-bank districts of Parione, Regola, Sant'Angelo (including the ghetto). Not long after, running water was also laid on as far as the fountain in Piazza Navona. In 1610–12 the refurbished aqueduct was

THE FONTANA PAOLA OR "FONTANONE"

The ambitious and costly enterprise of overhauling the aqueduct originally built by Emperor Trajan was already underway in 1610, when the papal engineers carried out the first tests and the pope ordered an imposing terminus to be built on the Janiculum alongside the church of San Pietro in Montorio, an architectural landmark that would be visible from everywhere in the city.

The *mostra d'acqua* was built in 1610–12 to designs by Domenico Fontana and Flaminio Ponzio, and inspired by the so-called Moses fountain celebrating the Acqua Felice. The Fontanone superseded its predecessor in size and beauty, however, as the triumphal three-arched layout was augmented to comprise two smaller, lateral arches. The marble was largely plundered from the Temple of Minerva in the Forum of Nerva. Moreover, four of the six columns of the fountain's frontage once graced the facade of the earlier Vatican basilica.

The dragons and eagles emblazoned on the upper extremities are elements from the Borghese family insignia. The two angels on either side of the central shield were sculpted by Ippolito Buzio in 1610. The inscription is of particular interest, as it points out the mistaken premise of the Acqua Paola: the pope and his engineers were misled into thinking that they

had restored the Aqua Alsietina, built under Augustus. The dedication also makes the hyperbolic claim that the water brought to Rome via the restored system was "saluberrima," i.e., eminently health-giving; actually its waters are only used for irrigation, industry, and for piping water to other fountains.

Originally the lower part of the fountain comprised five smaller basins, each fed by its own spout; in 1690 Carlo Fontana replaced them with the vast basin that can be seen today. Under Pope Innocent XII (r. 1691–1700), Monsignor Paolo Borghese had the basin cordoned off with a row of low marble posts, and another fountain set up in the nearby Botanical Gardens, to ensure the water was not fouled by animals using it as a trough.

But the main hazard was not so much the animals as the Romans themselves, who developed a habit of using this convenient pool of fresh water for washing their vegetables in the summer, and even for bathing. In 1707 a public order was issued prohibiting the fountain's use for such ablutions. Although the ordinance was reissued sporadically over the years, it was to little or no avail. Even today, on a hot afternoon, one can frequently see people cooling themselves off in the fountain's waters.

Opposite
The Fontanone of the Acqua Paola on the Janiculum.

embellished with a monumental terminus on the Janiculum, the Fontana Paola (known fondly as the Fontanone), and proceeded thence to the Ponte Sisto, to a second terminus, the Fontana di Ponte Sisto; this once stood at the junction of the bridge with Via Giulia, but was transferred in 1898 to Piazza Trilussa, on the right bank.

With admirable collective foresight, from the mid-sixteenth century to the first decade of the seventeenth various popes (Pius IV, Pius V, Gregory XIII, Sixtus V, Paul V) championed the revival of Rome's water system. The three major aqueducts (Virgo, Felice, Paolo) offered plentiful water all across Rome, endorsing the city's greatness and its claim as the hub of Catholicism and capital of the State of the Church. These sovereign pontiffs chose water as one of the principal motifs for propagandizing the redevelopment of the *urbs pontificum*. Indeed, the baroque city would be unthinkable without its fountains and water displays. They were a delight not only to the eye – witness the aerial linkage between the two terminuses of the Acqua Paola on the Janiculum, providing a spectacular backdrop to Via Giulia – but also to the ear: the sound of water gushing into the basins of marble and granite is a memorable feature of many corners of the city, and equally as characteristic as the sight of the city's obelisks.

In the space of half a century, between Pius IV and Paul V, the inhabitants of Rome grew familiar with the terminuses and monumental fountains marking the aqueducts, together with those set into the walls of buildings such as the hospitals of Santo Spirito, San Giacomo, San Rocco, and so forth. Alongside these were countless *fontanili* or utility fountains and drinking troughs for the great many horses and beasts of burden that passed through the streets. Water was also the essential source of power for the pre-industrial city. An eloquent testimony to this bygone landscape is the famous photograph of what was once Piazza Scossacavalli, with its fountain and drinking trough.

By the first few decades of the seventeenth century the papal city's water supply system was fully consolidated. But until as late as 1870 – when the Church's temporal powers over Rome dissolved – the papal authorities continued to boost the system's overall delivery capacity (at the end of the 1600s the Acqua Paola's output was increased by channeling in water from Lake Bracciano), improving and enlarging the pipelines both underground and above ground, together with the raised aqueducts, and defending the system from unauthorized use. Each operation followed the steady rise in the city's population and hence the growing need for public watering places and direct pipage into the private houses.

The two priorities were, naturally, the general supply to the public, and the architectural fountains. But the aqueducts also continued to provide the essential hydraulic power for the numerous industrial activities across the *urbs*, such as flourmills, textile works, spinning works, paper factories, ironsmiths, rope makers, and so forth. This industrial use of water was central to the intentions of Pope Innocent XIII (1721–24) when in 1723 he ordered two new freshwater springs to be routed into the twelfth-century aqueduct known as the *marrana* (or *marana*).

The water supply was vital to the dozens of mills and factories studding the built-up area within the city walls, from San Sisto Vecchio to the Circus Maximus and Santa Maria in Cosmedin. On the other hand, again in 1856, Pius IX instructed the *marana* to be linked up to the spring in Ciampino (discovered during excavation work for a tunnel for the Rome–Frascati railroad line), because the Circus Maximus, gasometer, and the *marana* were destined to become the "industrial areas" in the last twenty years of papal dominion.

After the prodigal enhancements made to the city's water system in the sixteenth and seventeenth centuries, little more was done on such a scale. The conduits were of course improved, and the clay piping replaced with modern lead ducts; the delivery capacity itself was increased, but, all in all, most of the city's water continued to come from the three main aqueducts, supplemented by the wells and springs (particularly those on the slopes of the Janiculum, among which were the Lancisiana, Pia, Innocenziana, San Damaso, and Api or Angelica).

It was during this phase of the city's history that Rome became renowned for the splendor and sheer number of its fountains. Toward the end of the sixteenth century, it became an expression of benevolence to build a public fountain (usually in the center of the piazza opposite one's residence, though on occasion attached to the family mansion itself). Such gestures of public largesse were encouraged by the papacy and were considered a due gift in acknowledgment of the papal bestowal of the privilege of running water in the family domicile. Moreover, it was less onerous to build a public fountain than to erect a church or family chapel. For this reason, an increasing number of families among the Roman aristocracy (which had entertained a scheme for closing its ranks to outsiders via the introduction of blood ties and a "golden book") began to shirk their responsibilities to the city's religious beautification, and limit their contribution to a family chapel, lodged within one of the main existing places of worship.

While monumental fountains were an ostensible token of the financial and political power of a given dynasty, the terminuses marking the end of an aqueduct tacitly remained the reserve of the uppermost echelons – a role the papacy awarded itself as a means of endorsing a supremacy that had endured unquestioned since the 1300s. And indeed, the sixteenth century saw the start of numerous papal schemes for enhancing the Aqua Virgo, which had been reactivated by Pope Nicholas V the previous century. Among the many schemes put forward during the baroque period – in which Rome's brilliant architect Gianlorenzo Bernini was the foremost exponent – was the Fontana di Trevi, created on the pope's express behest and surely one of the archetypal symbols of the city under the papacy.

As for the *mostre* terminuses for the Felice and Paola aqueducts, over a century later the predominant symbolism was still the triumphal arch, taking its cue once again from the said Trophies of Marius.

THE FONTANA DI TREVI

When Pius IV sanctioned improvements to the Aqua Virgo aqueduct, the project included the creation of a new fountain. It seems that when, in 1563, the young Giacomo Della Porta measured the basin installed upon the wish of his patron, Pope Nicholas V, and discovered it was not perfectly square (it measured 8.33 by 8.77 cm), he did nothing about it, despite being still officially engaged on the project in 1564.

In the ensuing century the fountain is recorded as still facing the Via del Corno; at its left side stood a drinking trough for animals. Later, in the course of improvements to the road network in the neighborhood under Paul V (1605–23), it became necessary to alter the fountain's basin.

When Giovanni Vasanzio put forward a project for redesigning the fountain, emulating the design of the terminus of the Acqua Felice aqueduct, his proposal was turned down by the Curia. In 1640 Gianlorenzo Bernini designed a new fountain, obtaining from Urban VIII (r. 1623–44) permission to cannibalize materials from the huge drum-shaped tomb of Cecilia Metella on the Via Appia Antica. The city council swiftly objected, but Bernini meanwhile proceeded to demolish the remains of the fountain that had been built in the fifteenth century. Though he reinstated the basin that is visible today, the *mostra d'acqua* remained unfinished because he was eventually denied authorization to take the marble from the Roman tomb.

In the decades that followed, Bernini remained hopeful of working on the Trevi area, and even proposed transporting the Trajan Column to the piazza to enliven the setting. Other architects were also dreaming up new projects, but none of them ever received the pontifical consent. The same thing happened in the following century when, in 1728, Pope Benedict XIII (r. 1724–30) instructed Paolo Benaglia to continue work on the fountain – this time supposedly conclusive – which was halted by the death of his patron two years later.

In 1732 work began on the definitive fountain. The task was entrusted by Clement XII (r. 1730–40) to the architect Nicola Salvi. Though unfinished, in 1735 the monument was given a preliminary inauguration; work was resumed after 1751 under the direction of Giovanni Paolo Pannini; the finished work was finally opened in 1762 by Pope Clement XIII (r. 1758–69).

The fountain as we know it today is slightly different from Salvi's original design, though he can be safely credited with the overall concept of this glorious monument. The building along whose side wall the fountain is set, Palazzo Poli, was begun in 1573 and later extensively reworked and joined to the existing buildings

Following pages
The Trevi fountain.

Details of the lithe sculptural figures from the Trevi fountain.

The imposing figure set in the elegant colonnaded niche (left and top) and one of the sculpted panels from the central portico composition.

around it; construction work continued even after the installation of the Trevi fountain. This backdrop enabled Salvi to give his imagination a free rein and create a complex and ingenious architectural setting.

Beneath the central triumphal arch with its four engaged columns on pilasters is an attic story with allegorical figures carved by Bartolomeo Pincellotti, Francesco Queirolo, Bernardino Ludovisi, and Agostino Corsini. The central inscription surmounted by the fastigium with the insignia of Clement XII flanked by two *Fames* is by Paolo Benaglia. The symmetrical wings on either side of the arch comprise a colossal order framing two stories of elegant balustraded windows with pediments.

On a rock in the central coffered exedra a statue representing the Ocean rides a shell-shaped carriage drawn by sea horses ridden by tritons, sculpted by Pietro Bracci in 1759–62.

The side niches enclose *Salubrity* (right), by Filippo della Valle, surmounted by *The Virgin indicating the spring to some soldiers*, by Andrea Bergondi; *Abundance* (left), by della Valle, is surmounted by *Agrippa approving the design of the aqueduct*, by G. B. Grossi.

The composition is completed by sculptures of rocks and petrified vegetation (after Bernini). This occupies the entire base of the palace and spills into the pond, with its raised borders representing the sea.

The Trevi fountain, which was restored in 1989–91, has always attracted crowds thanks to a popular legend by which anyone who drank from its waters could be sure to return to Rome. Nowadays, people do not drink from the fountain, but throwing in a coin supposedly does the trick. The fountain ranks alongside the Colosseum as one of Rome's best-loved symbols, and has appeared in numerous films.

The Trevi fountain is a triumph of virtuoso aquatic inventiveness. This grandiose theatrical monument, which so ingeniously espouses nature and culture, is matched by another gigantic set-design involving water, namely the Ripetta (1702), a former port on the bank of the Tiber which epitomized another of the main functions of water in Rome, together with the city's close ties with the river – a river that continued to be an indispensable lifeline, even though the heyday of the guild of *acquaroli* or water-carriers was long past.

As noted earlier, while the appointment of the *Magistri aedificiorum et stratarum* (a title that underwent many slight adjustments over time) signified the existence of an official body entrusted with the tutelage and maintenance of the aqueduct – and with preventing its misuse – the constant rise in demand for water in the ensuing century made the city's supply system an issue of primary civic importance. After the construction and renovation of the papal aqueducts, a new civil commission was set up, the Presidenza degli Acquedotti Urbani, whose main task was not so much to build new conduits or restore working order to the existing system, as to curb abuses of the network and put a halt to unauthorized connections (or connections that could overburden the system). Throughout the seventeenth century three separate bodies were responsible for overseeing the city's water supply, respectively for the Virgo, Felice, and Paola aqueducts. It was not until 1701 that Clement XI (r. 1700–21) united the two commissions for the Acqua Paola and Aqua Virgo; later, in 1742, Pope Benedict XIV grouped all three departments under a single commission.

In 1744 Benedict's engineers connected new springs up to the Aqua Virgo aqueduct, and a stricter system was devised for exacting water rates from consumers to cover the mounting supply and maintenance costs of the city's waterworks. The appeal was opposed vehemently by certain groups of the community, however, who claimed that in the past the supply had been freely donated by the papacy. The beneficiaries of the three aqueducts were divided into two categories: the "possessors" of the supply (namely, those who had received the supply as a gift, or had paid for it and were therefore taxed for this "private" water both at source and in supplementary tariffs), and the mere "consumers" (who liberally made use of the water available from the public fountains, and those who "rented" a specified quantity of water, without actually buying it).

After the turmoil of the Napoleonic period, Pope Pius VII (r. 1800–23) promulgated a general overhaul to the system of aqueducts, and in 1818 altered the method by which people were taxed on water consumption, together with the system of custody and repair of the network of aqueducts. The new setup distinguished the "public waterworks" (to be shouldered by the state treasury) from the "private waterworks" (to be

Overleaf
A dramatic, street-level view of the Trevi fountain.

paid by the end-users). However, the consumers opposed any form of taxation, citing documents dating back to the seventeenth century, and many claimed an amnesty for cases of unauthorized connection that had been in function for years.

For many centuries there had been no provision of water to the upper stories of the buildings on higher ground, nor to the rented upper floors of the taller buildings in the lower neighborhoods, particularly as regards the supply to individual apartments. The effect of this on personal hygiene and hence on the living standards of most of the lower-middle and working classes can be imagined. People were mistrustful of water, thinking that it was detrimental to the body's natural defenses, and consequently "waterless hygiene" was in widespread practice.

And such was the custom in the preindustrial city – and in Rome, the capital of the Church State – through until the mid-nineteenth century. The advances in technology themselves seem to have deterred any return to the ancient custom of public bathing. Fourteen centuries passed before public baths were reintroduced, under Benito Mussolini.

Despite their historiated frescoes and stucco work, many of the superb noble palazzi throughout the city were lacking proper toilet facilities. Running water on the *piano nobile* or upper story was an impossibility, and fully fitted bathrooms a great rarity. Water was normally lugged about by the household servants, whose living quarters were relegated to the building's uppermost stories.

In seventeenth-century Rome many palazzi, villas, and apartment blocks were available for rent. For practical purposes, architects were required to design apartment blocks in which the kitchens were as close as possible to the water supply, and therefore situated them over the courtyard well to enable the occupants to draw water directly from it with the appropriate mechanisms. These tenement blocks, and particularly the smarter ones designed for "gentlemen," consisted of one apartment per story; the toilet facilities (without running water) gave onto the stairs, or were fitted with a tube, complete with a stopper, into which chamber pots were emptied. Only later, in the eighteenth century, were toilet facilities located in separate rooms of their own, with suitable ventilation; alternatively, they were assigned to the *mignani* (from the Latin *maenianum* or projecting upper story) over the court or back yard. In the second half of the eighteenth century the city's streets and highways department had the duty to oversee the construction of new tenement blocks, but also issued permits to connect house drains up to the sewer main.

During this same period, in the lower quarters, piped water was laid on in many courtyards (as late as 1741, however, despite the apparent abundance of the water in the Trevi fountain, one of the taverns in Via Paolina – now Via del Babuino – was equipped with nothing but a fountain, a washtub, and a well in the courtyard), and even some upper stories began to receive running water.

By the mid-eighteenth century the papal city's public water network was one of its prized features. But the crowning moment came at the start of the following century, when the aqueducts were included in the monumental reorganization of Piazza del Popolo and the Pincio hill by the architect and town-planner Giuseppe Valadier (1762–1839).

Under the new pope, Pius IX (r. 1846–78), the industrial revolution finally reached Rome, but it proceeded from the top and worked its way down. One of Pius IX's most memorable endeavors in this direction was to foster the development of the railways, despite their having been condemned as anathema by his predecessor. In little to no time the district railroad caused drastic changes in the urban transport system. The former sea and river transport services were no longer economically viable, and in the last fifteen years of the papacy's temporal power the Tiber's erstwhile role as the great lifeline of commercial traffic to and from the sea and the interior dwindled to nothing.

In the last years of papal dominion a new phenomenon emerged, which would become a pivotal feature of the Third Rome, the Rome of the Italian Republic: the Tiber was embanked below the Lungotevere, drastically altering the relationship between the city and its river. This spelled doom for the picturesque mills along the water's borders, and made the numerous riverside quays and loading wharves, including the Ripa

Following pages
More views and details of the Trevi fountain.

Previous page
Central group and detail of the Naiad fountain.

Grande and Ripetta, reduntant. Once the Tiber was walled in, Rome ceased to be an "aquatic city," and turned its back on the river forever.

In 1865, a few years before the expiry of the papacy's temporal power, Pius IX authorized repairs – or, better, the construction *ex novo* – of the ancient Aqua Marcia system, to be carried out by a private corporation (similar to the commissions for the iron bridges over the Tiber). The decisive innovation in this case was the introduction of cast-iron piping enabling greater water-pressure through the system.

On the afternoon of Saturday, September 10, 1870, the ruling pontiff solemnly inaugurated the new terminus of the aqueduct, called the Acqua Pia, which was situated between the Termini railroad station and the Baths of Diocletian, opposite Palazzo Massimo, near the corner of Via Viminale. Ten days later, the Royalists stormed Porta Pia, putting an end to the papal domination of Rome, and the city passed into the hands of the Kingdom of Italy. A wry saying from those weeks of struggle runs: "Porta Pia, ieri tua, oggi mia," meaning "Porta Pia, yours yesterday, mine today."

Central jet of the Naiad fountain.

Opposite
One of the naiads.

THE ACQUA PIA TERMINUS, THE FONTANA DELLE NAIADI

The Acqua Pia water corporation had pledged to build the *mostra terminale* for the new aqueduct. By 1879 work had long overshot the three-year contract stipulated in the papal concession of 1865, but the first attempt had been found inept and inappropriate.

From a simple circular concave basin set on the ground rose a corona of modest sprays; at the center of the basin emerged a jet more powerful than the others.

The Town Plan of 1883 envisaged driving a new street through the old fabric, Via Nazionale. It was therefore decided to build a more imposing aqueduct terminus in line with the new thoroughfare. The engineer Alessandro Guerrieri was engaged to transfer the fountain to the center of Piazza Esedra, and the new composition was bulkier than its precursor: a large central section raised one meter above the pavement level was surrounded by four low semicircular basins, and the entire composition was enclosed in an iron railing.

The construction work was completed in 1885–89, and the question was raised of the new fountain's ornamentation. At first the consensus was for four lions on the platforms; some preferred sphinxes, however. In 1885 the special commission turned down a design with lions, and proposed instead four prone naiads, but for many years the right sculptor to execute the work could not be found.

In 1897 the commission chose Mario Rutelli. Without leaving his home town of Palermo, Rutelli began work on the casts of the four statuary groups that adorn the fountain today: each naiad reclines on an aquatic creature symbolizing water in its various forms: a sea horse for the oceans, a water-snake for the rivers, a swan for the lakes, and a peculiar reptile for the underground streams.

At the end of the 1900s the casts arrived in Rome and the council of Catholic ministers immediately pounced on the mayor for his decision to expose these scantily clad females, insisting they be replaced with lions. The maneuver was purely political, as nobody had ever objected to the equally naked naiads in the fountain at the north end of Piazza Navona. In truth, Rutelli's statues were merely a pretext to attack the council, and the councilors shrewdly opted to allow the public to decide for itself.

The inauguration ceremony was organized for the evening, and a crowd was expected. A ploy was invented to avoid revealing the naked naiads to the innocent eyes of the children. As it happened, the turnout was low, and the question had been greatly overplayed. Those invited to the inauguration did not find the naiads shameful and the composition was generally appreciated.

At any event, the public did decided for itself. On February 10, 1901, the last Sunday of carnival week, a group of people that had gathered near the fence screening the sculptures from view unceremoniously tore it down. The sculptor himself, who was boarding at the nearby Quirinale pension, was brought down to the site.

But the controversy was by no means over. In the years that followed, various self-elected spokespersons for public decency continued to canvass for the removal of Rutelli's statues, but in vain. On the contrary, the Palermo-born sculptor was actually awarded the commission for the fountain's centerpiece. For this, Rutelli at first designed a group composed of three tritons, a dolphin, and a giant octopus. The result was not accepted, however, and the locals jokingly dubbed the work "fritto misto" (a mixed seafood fry-up). So the council invited the sculptor to withdraw his work and replace it with something more appropriate.

In 1911 the centerpiece of the fountains was finally installed. It comprised a five-meter portrait of the sea-god Glaucus clasping a dolphin from whose mouth a powerful jet of water streaks skyward. The statue is supposed to represent man's dominion over the brute forces of nature. The Glaucus figure was immediately more popular than the "fritto misto" and has commanded its position ever since; its predecessor languishes in a sort of dried-up pond in the gardens of Piazza Vittorio Emanuele, where it has quickly decayed, blending with the far more ancient pieces of antiquity populating the piazza. The popularity of the sea-god, referred to locally as "the man with the fish," increased when it

was learned that Rutelli's model was the writer of satirical verse in Roman dialect, Trilussa (alias Carlo Alberto Salustri), a man renowned for his imposing physique. As late as the 1940s, during the war years, one could still occasionally witness schoolchildren trooping through the square, instructed by their teachers to look in the other direction.

The terminal fountain of the Acqua Pia Antica Marcia, to cite its full name, forged a new genre that would enjoy popularity in the second half of the century. The scheme consisted of offsetting a display of dancing water against an architectural backdrop, which took the place of the once popular triumphal arch composition.

Details from the Naiad fountain.

Opposite
The centerpiece, featuring the sea-god Glaucus.

~ 65 ~

THE THIRD ROME

In 1870 the city's population had reached 226,000, and the built-up area was a lush sea of greenery, some carefully tended and some left to its own devices. Villas, garden plots, pasture, undeveloped lots, made way for the sprawling urbanization as the physical city grew to accommodate the rising population. In the space of a few decades the antique city known as the "papalina" or papal city was totally engulfed. The three oldest among the city's aqueducts delivered around 150,000 cubic meters of water per day. The waters of the Acqua Pia Antica Marcia (its name aggrandized to suit the current tastes of the liberal ruling class) were channeled into dozens of high-pressure iron conduits, and the system was equipped with pumping stations enabling a greater throughput of purer water supplied throughout the city.

Within a few decades the Pia Antica Marcia aqueduct made urbanization possible on all the hills of Rome, including the areas outside the old city walls. The new high-pressure cast-iron piping finally guaranteed flowing water to the rental accommodation on the upper floors of buildings everywhere.

The improvements to the aqueduct also brought a general betterment of standards in personal hygiene. The availability of running water in both the old and the new city upset the customs and habits of the population, altering the frequency and way in which it performed its daily ablutions. The old marble washbowl of yore with its wrought-iron stand and array of jugs and buckets was gradually ousted by the purpose-built washbasin installed in a room of its own. Similarly, the zinc bathtub and hip-baths (filled and emptied by hand) yielded to the properly equipped bath with drain.

The enhanced aqueducts and sewerage heralded the arrival of the proper flushing water-closet, either installed separately or in an enclosure on the back balcony of the tenement blocks, to take advantage of the distribution pipes and public drainage network. The local Roman term for the balcony "out-house" usually fitted with a "Turkish" or standing closet, or a tube with appropriate stopper (the very earliest of conveniences for the lower classes) was *mignanello*, from the term *maenianum* used in republican Rome. The somewhat blunt alternative was and still is simply *cesso*, short for *necessarium*.

The new aqueduct – the last of those built by the papacy – provided the necessary thrust to the physical expansion and population growth of the city. Water was an even more important commodity than speculation capital, and was considered a fundamental feature of civilized housing across Europe. The Acqua Pia Antica Marcia corporation found itself with a virtual monopoly, and was the focus of countless deals and policies involving both Italian and foreign capital, not to mention the local government bodies, and private interests (clergy, aristocracy, *nouveaux riches*, and so on), and entrepreneurs from the north.

This monopoly was not affected by the municipal body controlling the three oldest papal aqueducts, as their overall delivery capacity was far inferior to that of the Acqua Pia's main duct, which in 1886 supplied no less than 1,200–1,500 liters per second of eminently potable water. The monopoly survived the Fascist era, notwithstanding the

The N.A.V.E. terminus below the Pincio terrace in Piazza del Popolo.

Opposite
A corner of the Lion fountain in Piazza del Popolo, seen against the terminus of the N.A.V.E. corporation aqueduct below the Pincio terrace.

new central governorship's notorious inflexibility. Upon the expiry of the ninety-nine years' concession (1865–1964) accorded by Pope Pius IX, the monopoly had seen its way through four different political types of authority: those of the papacy, the Liberals, the Fascists, and the new Democratic Republicans.

In the years that followed the storming of Porta Pia (1870), work proceeded on the three papal aqueducts, heralding improvements that have continued until recent years, and leading to the creation of a fully integrated water mains that enables water to be channeled from all the city's aqueducts in every direction.

At the end of the nineteenth century the construction of the pumping station in Piazza del Popolo (completed in 1901) greatly increased the pressure and capacity of the Aqua Virgo. In addition to improving the network as a whole, attempts were made to partially modify the distribution into each building, with the installation of water meters together with the regulating valves for service tanks, usually fitted on the terrace of each building.

In 1909–10 another important pumping station was built for the Aqua Virgo, boosting its capacity to around 500 liters per second. Built in 19 B.C., the venerable aqueduct was in its dotage, and required constant repairs and maintenance. Consequently, during the governorship of Francesco Boncompagni Ludovisi (1928–35) it was decided to embark on the construction of a new system, the Nuovo Acquedotto Vergine Elevato (N.A.V.E.), which would mark a new technological departure. The system was equipped with a pumping station at the source in Salone, a piezometric tower, cast-iron piping for water under pressure, a large reservoir in the Villa Borghese gardens (linked up to the ancient reserve of San Sebastianello) and a terminal fountain, which was completed in 1936–37.

THE TERMINAL FOUNTAIN FOR THE NUOVO ACQUEDOTTO VERGINE ELEVATO

The new fountain for the N.A.V.E. was built to designs by Valadier, who at the turn of the previous century had envisaged a large fountain with cascades and water-jets set into the retaining wall at the foot of the Pincio terraces; the idea was to provide a sort of an elevated counterpart to the three fountains in Piazza del Popolo. Valadier's imprint is unmistakable in the twentieth-century design, as can be seen from the photographs, which show the fountains of the square set against the *mostra d'acqua* at the foot of the Pincio.

Together with the ancient Aqua Virgo, the new supply system was capable of delivering 1,500 liters of supply water per second. As a result of further enchancements in 1966–78, the rate of certified drinking water has reached 800 liters per second.

While the Aqua Virgo has somewhat dwindled in importance in recent years, the Acqua Paola has fared much worse, and for a long time it was not a proper potable supply. Work on the system has been going on for decades, but it was nonetheless only used for supplying street fountains, watering lawns and gardens, and for industrial purposes. Its delivery capacity in 1943 was only 500 liters per second. After World War II the general overhaul of the city's waterworks involved extensive modifications to the network, including the installation of a purification station at Pineta Sachetti (where since 1968 the supply has been mixed with that of the Peschiera aqueduct), and a second purification plant at Grottarossa, which has made it possible to draw water from the Tiber itself since 1970–78.

Another papal aqueduct that has remained in the shadows is Pope Sixtus V's Acqua Felice, which was channeled into the Acqua Pia Antica Marcia; its throughput is relatively meager by comparison; in 1943 it delivered a mere 250 liters per second. Subsequently it was superseded by the new Appio-Alessandrino aqueduct.

While the history of the papal water supply systems was fraught with changes and overhauls, the said Appio-Alessandrino aqueduct has also required regular alterations and enlargements (indeed, work began in 1868 and did not end until 1970, in time for Rome's centenary celebrations as the capital of unified Italy).

The N.A.V.E. terminus with its commanding statue of the goddess Roma, framed against the arches of the Pincio terrace.

The year 1898 saw the inauguration of the second aqueduct of the Acqua Pia Antica Marcia system, which boasted a delivery capacity of some 2,500 liters per second. Despite its notable throughput, however, by 1924–28 it became necessary to replace all the piping of the system's primary aqueduct (functioning since 1870), and increase its load to 3,500 liters per second. Between 1918 and 1937 extensive hydraulic engineering work was carried out to harness five new freshwater sources to cope with the rising demand among the population, which by this time had reached the figure of one million.

The two mainline aqueducts of the Acqua Pia Antica Marcia received their water from the sources in the outlying borough of Tivoli, and conveyed it to the capital in high-pressure cast-iron siphons. The water corporation actually built another four aqueducts in the years from 1870 to 1907, and a further three in 1923–37. In 1943 the seven siphons of the water mains were delivering no more than 4,500 liters per second, out of a potential capacity of 6,000. Frankly, the network was antiquated, and despite having been extensively patched up over the years, it was leaking everywhere. Despite their state of disrepair, the corporation was reluctant to incur further financial outlay, and kept its eye on the profits.

After World War II further work was carried out to make use of the various untapped springs and sources, as the Acqua Pia Antica Marcia had to shoulder the soaring demand for running water from the rapidly expanding built-up area. Once the papal water concession had expired, in 1964 the A.C.E.A. was in a position to build an extra siphon, bringing the overall yield of the system up to the required 6,000 liters per second, a capacity that had been technically feasible since the 1930s.

As the capital steadily grew into a modern metropolis, the city's complex water system was greatly enhanced by the addition of water from the Peschiera and Capore aqueducts. This enlargement marked the decisive phase in the supply of water to the affluent industrial city, in which the indiscriminate use of water is perhaps one of the basic attributes of a modern consumer society.

Although the engineering project for the Peschiera aqueduct dates from 1913, work did not actually get under way until 1935, and was suspended during the war years. Resumed in 1947, the undertaking was finally completed in 1980.

THE PESCHIERA TERMINUS

In the Republican-Democratic period, too, the need arose for a *mostra terminale* to mark the water corporation's activities and celebrate the inauguration of a new aqueduct.

In light of the coming Holy Year, the first since World War II, the city council commissioned a new monumental fountain to adorn Piazza degli Eroi, marking the terminus of the Peschiera aqueduct.

In the center of a large circular tub rose a composite octagonal structure flanked by smaller pools of semicircular shape. The long sides of the octagon, embellished with spurting shells, alternate with other cascades set into the shorter sides. At the top a broad shallow basin carries the main, leaping jet of water.

In this case there was no architectural backdrop, unlike the papal terminuses. Perhaps there was no need – in itself the composition provides a spectacular display of water, illuminated at night to great effect.

Furthermore, unlike the superb fountain designed by Rutelli for Piazza dell'Esedra, the new *mostra* is completely lacking in statuary or sculpture. Basically, the architecture takes a back seat, leaving the water to speak for itself.

The terminus of the Peschiera aqueduct, and the ornamental fountain of the Peschiera-Capore waterworks.

The water from the Peschiera aqueduct was first channeled into the city in 1949, with the inauguration of the new fountain in Piazzale degli Eroi, and the new abundant supply greatly boosted the urbanization of many neighborhoods. In 1961 the Capore springs were also piped into the network; this additional system vaunted all the latest technology, with conduits in steel and prestressed reinforced concrete, and a central operations console for monitoring the entire system electronically. In recent years this system has taken the lion's share of the city's water supply; in 1980 it vaunted a capacity of no less than 14,000 liters per second.

THE ORNAMENTAL FOUNTAIN
OF THE PESCHIERA-CAPORE AQUEDUCTS

In 1961 the square in front of the headquarters of the A.C.E.A. was embellished with a new fountain serving as the terminus for the new aqueduct network known by the name of Peschiera-Capore. The fountain drew on the new tradition introduced by its twin for the Acqua Pia Antica Marcia. Again there was no architectural backdrop, and no sculptures, just a superb display of water.

From 1963 to 1968 a highly modern aqueduct was built, stretching from the borough of Pantano Borghese. The new Appio-Alessandrino system harnessed water from the earlier Acqua Felice aqueduct, and was built principally to serve the southeastern sector of the city. Although the system claims a capacity of only 1,200 liters per second, and is linked up to the Acqua Pia Antica Marcia, it nonetheless performs a vital role in the system as a whole, and involves high-tech impounding wells, pumping and distribution stations, steel mains, and remote control systems that set it apart from the Peschiera-Capore system.

In the postwar years the supply of drinking water to Rome was increased to keep apace with a demographic boom that continued unchecked all through the 1970s. In 1955 the various aqueducts vaunted an overall capacity of 14,500 liters per second. In 1980 this was raised to 23,400 liters per second, a part of which (800 l/s) is not potable.

The increase in the aqueducts' delivery capacity (especially the Peschiera-Capore system) has guaranteed adequate supply not only to the official quarters of the city, but even to the neighborhoods that have materialized through unauthorized building. As a consequence, the standard of living in the *borgate* or outlying boroughs was greatly ameliorated. The real revolution in water supply at this stage was the terrific surge in water usage caused by the introduction of showers and domestic appliances such as dishwashers and washing-machines. The increase in consumption was part and parcel of a general improvement in lifestyle, even for the lower-paid classes, that had no comparison in the earlier years of the industrial revolution, nor even with the thriving decades from 1870 to World War II – years in which the Roman capital experienced a particular boom.

At all events, the massive volumes of water transported via the new aqueducts and enhanced pressure mains continued to be reflected in new fountains for public enjoyment. From the days of the Liberals, through the years of the monarchy and into the Fascist era, to the modern Democratic-Republican age, fountains continued to be a central feature of Rome's urban furniture, even in the more far-flung neighborhoods outside the walls.

On occasion, the fountains' designs harked back to models that were popular in earlier days. Generally, however, architects tended to give free rein to their imagination. Fine examples are the Fontana delle Rane in Piazza Mincio (in which the designer Gino Coppedé gave a baroque cast to his work), and the numerous street fountains designed by Pietro Lombardi (each of which incorporates the emblems of the specific neighborhood: books for the Sapienza quarter, paintbrushes for Via Margutta, the "artists" quarter; and *amphorae* for the Testaccio quarter). Some of the city's more recent fountains are found in the "new" neighborhoods of the EUR district (formerly known as E42). They reflect a more modern approach, while remaining ever attentive to the classicizing idea of water as one of Rome's intrinsic and most typical features.

At little more than a century since the country's unification with Rome as its capital, the constant transformations across the city have seen the revival of what are jokingly known as "ballerina" fountains. Keenly aware of the legacy of this particular kind of monument in the city's history and landscape, architects, sculptors, planners, functionaries, and council engineers have unhesitatingly recycled fountains of earlier date, in many cases restoring and relocating them appropriately. Since the late nineteenth century, countless newspaper and magazine articles (and discussions in council offices) have focused on the retrieval of the many relics of fountains that have fallen prey to relentless expansion and urban redevelopment.

Such strong feelings are rooted in Rome's ancient claim to the title of *Regina Aquorum*, and later as the "city of fountains." The debate reached a peak in the pages of the review *Capitolium*, which carried vital contributions from eminent critics and scholars of architecture, such as Cesare D'Onofrio, Carlo Pietrangeli, and Armando Ravaglioli.

The fountain as a choice feature of the urban landscape, as one of Rome's distinguishing landmarks, was taken up in a recent well-publicized competition for the redevelopment of certain new piazzas in the outskirts of the city. The competition was announced in 1986 jointly by the municipal development department and the A.C.E.A.; in 1989 the latter body's headquarters mounted an exhibition of the winning projects. None of these has yet been actuated, however.

THE EYE OF THE CAMERA

Major Fountain Groups in Rome's Squares

S everal of Rome's squares have seen the aggregation of two or more fountains. This does not mean a composite structure comprising fountain, drinking trough, and washtub, but a full-fledged architectural grouping of elements. Such aggregations were unfailingly a byproduct of urban renewal schemes applied to some specific corner or zone of the city. As regards Piazza del Popolo, Piazza Navona, Saint Peter's Square, Piazza Farnese, and the Quattro Fontane intersection, here we will concentrate on the construction of the fountains, leaving out most references to the urban schemes under way at the time, an argument that lies outside the compass of this book.

The Fountains in Piazza del Popolo

From the end of the 1400s attempts had been made to exploit the scenic potential of the clearing near the city gate known as Porta del Popolo. But early the following century few improvements had been made, and the "square" remained an irregular, unpaved site.

The Medici pope, Leo X (r. 1513–21), ordered a bold and radical scheme for the redevelopment of the piazza and the main concourses leading into it, Via Lata (now Via del Corso) and the new Via Leonina (now Ripetta). The operation also implicated some of the side-streets, and fostered the emergence of a self-contained quarter encompassing the Ripetta river-port on the Tiber, Via Lata, and the said square at Porta del Popolo.

The second Medici pope, Clement VII, sponsored work on one of the axial streets into the square, rechristened Via Clementina in his honor (later renamed Via Paolina Trifaria, and now Via del Babuino). The new scheme involved reworking the *trivium* or fan of three streets that issue from the square opposite the city gate. In the mid-1500s this area was still very much a suburb, with grazing land and vineyards all around.

Despite the erection of Sixtus' obelisk in the center of the square in 1589, the site retained a decidedly unfinished and forlorn look, a situation that was only partially remedied in the following century with the construction of twin churches marking the convergence of the *trivium*. But the splendid remodeling of the city gateway and the three concourses serving the square (Via di Ripetta, Via del Corso, Via del Babuino) was not matched by a fitting architectural closure on the Tiber side, nor on the Pincio gardens side, opposite. Similarly, the center of the square itself had been left unfinished, in spite of the sixteenth-century fountain fed by the Aqua Virgo (the work was dubbed the "Trullo," or hut, owing to the presence of an ungainly stone vestige from some ancient building that once occupied the site).

In 1571 the trustees of the Capitoline water authority granted permission to take the water from the Trevi fountain to Piazza del Popolo. It was therefore decided to equip the square with a fountain, the first (1572) of the eighteen new fountains designed by Giacomo Della Porta, of which only nine were actually built and installed. It was soon observed that the new fountain was dwarfed by the square, and three years later a washing tub and drinking trough were added to Della Porta's composition. When the

The right sphinx of the Neptune fontain in Piazza del Popolo.

Opposite
One of the four lions of the central fountain in Piazza del Popolo.

Egyptian obelisk (12th or 13th cent. B.C.) was erected by order of Pope Sixtus V in the center of the square, one of Domenico Fontana's many spectacular accomplishments, the site's general lack of harmony became strikingly apparent. It was singularly unbecoming for one of the city's principal gateways.

In 1784 Giuseppe Valadier drafted a project for the piazza, but work was not completed until the following century. In 1811 the French occupation government decided to turn the untended slopes of the Pincio into elegant gardens for public enjoyment. The assignment was entrusted by the prefect Camille de Tournon to Giuseppe Valadier, who tendered a combined scheme for the hill and the square below. Work came to a halt with the fall of Napoleon and the end of French occupation, but was resumed in 1815–16, albeit with some small modifications to the original scheme. The square was ready by 1824, ingeniously framed by the elegant terracing of the Pincio above it.

Valadier's scheme involved the complete transformation of Piazza del Popolo, which was duly reconfigured with his distinctive neoclassical stamp. For its center, the architect summarily eliminated Della Porta's fountain, and instead surrounded the obelisk with four Egyptian-style lions reclining atop stepped pyramids. The water issuing from the mouth of each lion falls into a small circular basin (1823).

Bordering the piazza on either side of the "Trident" (the name given to the junction of the three thoroughfares) Valadier built two houses for the Torlonia family (the buildings that currently house the Café Rosati and Café Canova, occupying the corner site at Via di Ripetta and Via del Babuino respectively), while toward Via Flaminia he built a barracks for the Carabinieri (state police corps). On the opposing Tiber and Pincio flanks the architect created two monumental exedras, in the center of which stand two grand fountains adorned with sculpture groups. The sweeping bays of the two exedras are attributed to the French architects Alexandra-Jean-Baptiste Guy de Gisore and Louis Martin Berthault; the fountains were built to the designs of Valadier.

On the Pincio side of the piazza a sculpture group representing the goddess Roma looms over a shell-shaped fountain basin; at her sides sit the river-gods representing the Tiber and the Arno, while at her feet the she-wolf suckles the twins Romulus and Remus. The group is the work of Giovanni Ceccarini. The fountain on the opposite side is embellished with a Neptune group (comprising the water-god, two tritons, and two dolphins), again the work of Ceccarini.

The central lion fountain and those with Roma and Neptune did not exhaust the scheme envisaged by Valadier. He had planned that the backdrop afforded by the retaining wall beneath the Pincio terracing should be filled with a grand fountain or terminus set into niches. This was executed in 1937 (see section on the N.A.V.E. terminus). As one might expect, Valadier's idea drew pointedly on the triumphal arch motif.

One of the pairs of entwined dolphins from the Neptune fountain in Piazza del Popolo.

THE THREE FOUNTAINS IN PIAZZA NAVONA

Piazza Navona grew out of the ruins of the stadium built by Domitian in A.D. 81–96, on whose site in the Middle Ages countless oratorios, towers, and houses had sprouted. In the fifteenth century new palazzi and churches swallowed up the pre-existing structures, and transformed the former stadium's *platea* into a town square, which in 1577 housed the market of Campidoglio. The piazza assumed its current form in the seventeenth century.

Piazza Navona has long been one of Rome's favorite gathering places. In the seventeenth century it attracted an untold number of painters and etchers, and in the 1900s it was frequently used as a setting by film-makers.

Throughout the second half of the sixteenth century the popes repeatedly toyed with the idea of installing a fountain group, but it was not to come into being until the following century. Much of the piazza's appeal is due to the three fountains, which embody the changing styles in urban furniture, ranging from Della Porta to Bernini.

Opposite
The towering figure of the Neptune fountain on the west hemicycle in Piazza del Popolo.

*The imperious goddess Roma from the
fountain on the east hemicycle in
Piazza del Popolo, below the Pincio
gardens.*

Opposite
*Close-up of the Neptune figure from
the fountain on the west side of Piazza
del Popolo.*

Rear view of the central figure of the
Moor fountain in Piazza Navona.

Front view of the central figure of the
Moor fountain in Piazza Navona.

One of the shapely water-nymphs from the Neptune fountain in Piazza Navona.

THE FONTANA DEL MORO

The Moor fountain marks the indefatigable Della Porta's umpteenth installment of a multiple commission he reeived for new fountains all across Rome. In 1574 the architect subcontracted the creation of the basin from the Fiesole-born sculptor Ludovico Rossi; Rossi is recorded in 1576 as working on the secondary basins, the steps supporting them, and the travertine balusters and railing surrounding the fountain. The enclosure is no more, but appears in a drawing dated 1618.

In 1652–55 Rome's great baroque architect Gianlorenzo Bernini was called in to finish the fountain, and added some sculptures to the composition. At first he proposed a group that was quickly dubbed "The Snail," sculpted by Angelo Vannelli and composed of three dolphins with their tails entwined and a conch-shell over the top. However, the design was disliked and soon removed. In May 1653 the pontiff approved the design of the famous Moor composition, which Giovanni Antonio Mari had sculpted in Bernini's residence, where the architect could keep his eye on its progress. The Moor – actually just another triton figure, albeit inordinately large – was set in place in 1655. The previous year, however, Bernini had voiced his intentions to alter certain aspects of the fountain's design, and proceeded to remove the two steps beyond the baluster. Here he created a broad pool at ground level shaped to follow the profile of the main basin (in 1708, the renovator of the Aqua Virgo, G. B. Contini, replaced the pavonazzo rim with a border of white marble). At the end of the eighteenth century the tritons of the first fountain of Piazza del Popolo, demolished by Valadier, were added to this fountain. The tritons, restored in 1813, were copied by Luigi Amici in 1874 and, paradoxically, the ones in Piazza Navona are replicas – the originals were taken to Villa Borghese. The four other characters alternating with the tritons are original, however.

THE FONTANA DEL NETTUNO

Also known as the Fontana degli Calderari or coppersmiths (whose workshops stood nearby), the Neptune fountain was at first similar in structure to that of its counterpart on the southern side of the square, and the two were actually designed as a pair. As with the Fontana del Moro, Bernini removed the double step and the baluster railing to install a larger pool at ground level. In this case, however, the fountain remained unadorned for some time. (The four figures originally designed by Della Porta for this composition were used for the Pantheon fountain, as described in the relative section.) Furthermore, the Neptune fountain has none of the sculptural work Bernini proposed.

In 1873 the municipal council mounted a competition for the completion and decoration of the fountain locally known as "de' Calderaj." The jury's decision ignited a controversy. After some delay, in 1876 Antonio della Bitta submitted a life-size plaster working model of his proposal for the central group, consisting of Neptune struggling with a marine monster. Meanwhile, Giorgio Zappalà executed eight sketches for the side groups of nereids, putti, and sea horses. The compositions were applauded, and two years later the two winners delivered the works for which they had been commissioned.

THE FONTANA DEI FIUMI

The very earliest scheme for the supply of water to the square envisaged three fountains, and around 1575 a drinking trough was installed amid the so-called Moor and Neptune fountains. In 1645 the reigning pope, Innocent X (r. 1644–55), chose the square as the site for the forthcoming family mansion, and requested a grandiose fountain composition to render the square more suitable. This was to be the terminus for the Aqua Virgo, supplanting the existing terminus in Piazza Trevi. The pontiff therefore had the conduits in Piazza Navona modified, a task he entrusted to Bernini's jealous rival and almost exact contemporary, Francesco Borromini. In 1647 the pope had the Egyptian obelisk at the Circus of Maxentius on the Appian Way removed to Piazza Navona. And though Bernini had retreated somewhat into the background, he began work on a series of drawings for a circular fountain at the center of the said square, taking his cue from the Fontana delle Tartarughe, and gradually reaching the design we know today.

Part of the Moor fountain in Piazza Navona.

Opposite
Central figure from the Neptune fountain in Piazza Navona.

Various details from the Neptune fountain in Piazza Navona.

Details from the Rivers fountain in Piazza Navona.

Meanwhile, the pope had turned down Borromini's far simpler design, and in 1648 decided to pass the commission to Bernini. In August 1649 the obelisk envisaged by the latter's scheme was transferred to the site and erected upon a high base surmounted by a rugged pyramidal composition of sculpted marble, around which Bernini installed a complex allegory of the greatest rivers then known (Ganges, Danube, Nile, and Rio de la Plata). The four statues tower a good five meters high and were carved over the period May 1650 to July 1651 in compliance with Bernini's *bozzetti* (the Ganges statue is by Claude Poussin, the Danube by Antonio Raggi, the Plate by Francesco Baratta, and the Nile by Giovanni Maria Fracchi or Giacomo Antonio Fancelli). Likewise, the coat of arms of the Pamphilj family was completed according to Bernini's design.

The four main sculptures and the obelisk are surrounded by sea horses and sea-monsters sculpted by the said G. M. Fracchi. But the composition also comprises a lion, a water-snake, an armadillo, and two dolphins to symbolize the various fauna native to the zones traversed by the rivers in question. The task of coordinating the work was prodigious, but he received the sum of 4,000 *scudi*, 3,000 of which was paid in cash, and the remaining 1,000 for a knighthood conceded to his brother.

By 1651 the fountain was ready and, to celebrate, the pope issued permission for the square to be flooded, a device employed in Piazza Farnese also. This festive custom was repeated through until the end of the temporal power of the papacy, as testified by a photograph of 1865 and by the American poet Longfellow, who praised the scene as one of the gayest midsummer festivals of Rome.

The expenses for the laborious transportation of the Egyptian obelisk and the construction of the fountain were considerable, and the public resented the extra taxes levied upon them for the purpose. Moreover, in 1651 the pope attempted to rid the square of its long tradition as a street market for fruit and vegetables, rag-trade, book-sellers, second-hand sellers, and scrap-iron merchants. His efforts came to nothing. The market remained, and many years later, in 1858, the master of American fiction Nathaniel Hawthorne was able to note in his diary the colorful riot of little street-vendors' stalls.

THE TWO FOUNTAINS IN SAINT PETER'S SQUARE

For centuries successive popes had gradually enlarged the Emperor Constantine's complex of the Basilica of Saint Peter, making it the hub of a veritable citadel of ecclesiastical power. In the mid-1400s Pope Nicholas V (r. 1447–55) initiated the radical transformation of the existing basilica. Demolition began in 1452, but work on the new building was not taken in hand until early the following century (in 1506, under Julius II). Three hundred years later, in 1784, the bulk of the work was just nearing completion, and further additions and modifications were still under way at the end of the twentieth century even.

During this protracted period of construction, the entire area around today's magnificent basilica underwent extensive remodeling, including the creation of the huge square with its fountains and immense colonnade to create an enclosure screening the basilica from the nearby Borgo.

In 1490 Innocent VIII (r. 1484–92) had a fountain constructed whose design consisted of two superimposed basins, and was installed slightly to the right facing the basilica. During the pontificate of the Borgia pope, Alexander VI (r. 1492–1503), the fountain was restored by Alberto da Piacenza with the help of one of the basilica's earliest architects, Donato Bramante. The fountain was greatly admired for its size and the sheer abundance of its water flow; a third basin had been added, adorned with four gilt bronze bull-heads spouting water into the basin on the intermediate level. After the death of the Borgia pope the four bull-heads were replaced by four putti; a drinking-trough was set alongside, made from an earlier fountain basin, and emblazoned with the Borgia coat of arms.

Carlo Maderno demolished and rebuilt the fountain in 1614 when the Acqua Paola water was piped to the square. His elegant new design paid homage to the models of antiquity. At the center a capacious square basin rises on an octagonal pedestal bearing

Figures from the Rivers fountain in Piazza Navona.

The two monumental fountains in Saint Peter's Square.

the genealogical badge of Paul V, above which the water collects in a marble basin and thence descends into an upturned basin. The powerful central jet sends the water high into the air. On the octagonal base of the right-hand fountain one can still see the eagle and the Borgia emblems, commemorating the installation.

Bernini subsequently remodeled the square. His first move was to demolish Maderno's fountain and rebuild it, with a minor modification (1667), that is, moving it further to the right. The composition itself is set back one meter, while the lower basin was enlarged. That same year work began on a twin fountain on the left side of the square; it was completed ten years later, when the throughput of the Acqua Paola was increased. Carved in relief on the base of this fountain are two entwined dolphins, along with the coat of arms of the Altieri pope, Clement X. The colonnade, central obelisk, and two fountains helped transform the square of Saint Peter's into a "grand teatro dell'universo" (grand theater of the universe).

THE TWO FOUNTAINS IN PIAZZA FARNESE AND THE FOUNTAIN IN VIA GIULIA

In 1495 Cardinal Alessandro Farnese purchased a mansion standing between Campo dei Fiori (literally, Field of Flowers) and Via Giulia. In the ensuing decades he progressively bought up the adjacent lots, until, in 1523, he was in a position to commence work on a new residence for the dynasty. When the cardinal became Paul III in 1534 he determined to transform the building into a residence of more palatial dimensions. Through until the year 1589 the Farnese dynasty continued to pour money into the construction of the palace.

The building's construction involved the entire neighborhood, from the Via Giulia behind to the square at the front. In the space of a century the "Farnese neighborhood" was steadily consolidated, and became the hub of a district that was fast becoming the most fashionable in the city. As can be expected, the Farnese also intended to leave their imprint on the area's urban development, and to this end erected a fountain. In that age, providing a fountain was a customary *dono* or gift to the people on the part of the noble families. The Farnese's was to be installed in the square before the Palazzo Farnese (now the home of the French Embassy).

The two gray granite basins that form the base of the fountain in what is now Piazza Farnese were taken from the Baths of Caracalla, where they were discovered in the Middle Ages; Pope Paul III had had them transported to Piazza San Marco in Venice in 1466 to stand before his own palace. Thereafter, Paul III Farnese relocated them to their present site, raising them on a base. The other basin was brought to Piazza Farnese in 1580, as part of an exchange: Cardinal Odoardo Farnese offered to swap his for a basin in red porphyry that was found near Porta San Lorenzo, which Giacomo Della Porta immediately set alongside his patron's *palazzetto* in Venice. Much later it was transferred to the Pincio. The two basins initially fulfilled a solely ornamental role, without water. Under Paul III the first basin, installed centrally in the square, was used as a kind of spectator's tribune, high out of harm's way, during the horse-races held outside the palace. When Cardinal Farnese obtained the second basin the idea came to use them for a fountain, but the water pressure was as yet insufficient.

The two basins were not adapted for use as a fountain until 1626, as in 1621 Odoardo Farnese obtained from Pope Gregory XV 40 *once* of water siphoned from the *mostra* at the end of the Ponte Sisto, and was therefore in a position to prepare the necessary hydraulics for the two fountains. At this point the fountain was raised upon a large pool sculpted from travertine and adorned with a gigantic version of the Farnese emblem, the lily. A drawing executed in 1645 shows the two fountains in use for flooding the piazza, a popular amusement that was practiced for some time in Piazza Navona.

The end section of Via Giulia fell within the "Farnese" borough, as it were, and was linked up to the Tiber via a bridge beyond Via Giulia. A fountain was planned for a site not far from Palazzo Farnese in 1570 (though not actually built until 1626), and com-

The sculpted bases of the central elements of the Saint Peter's Square fountains.

The right fountain in Piazza Farnese.

Opposite (top)
*The twin right and left fountains
in Piazza Farnese.*

Opposite (bottom)
*The mascaron wall-fountain
in Via Giulia, with its distinctive
scallop basin and architectural volutes.*

The Four Fountains intersection: Diana (or Fidelity) and the Arno (or Aniene), respectively on the north and east corners.

Opposite
The fountain representing Juno (or Strength) at the west corner.

prised a large mascaron of white marble and a rectangular basin in porphyry, both carved during the days of ancient Rome.

Originally the fountain was not set against the wall, but stood in a small clearing. The travertine lily emblem, fixed to the crown of the group (replaced with an iron copy in the last century), stood as a token of the Farnese patronage.

THE FOUNTAINS AT VIA DELLE QUATTRO FONTANE AND VIA XX SETTEMBRE

Though brief, the pontificate of Sixtus V (1589–90) left an indelible mark on the city of Rome. In the five years of his rule the pontiff and his architect Domenico Fontana channeled their energies and ingenuity into redeveloping the city and its surroundings: new streets were driven through the old fabric of the city, old ones straightened and paved; old churches were renovated and new ones built; aqueducts were constructed and obelisks erected. And, of course, new fountains made their appearance too.

Sixtus' most significant contribution to Rome's urban planning was Via Felice, the street named after him, a spectacular straight thoroughfare nearly 3.5 kilometers long that bridged four hills (the Pincio, Quirinal, Viminal, and Esquiline), affording a quadruple view of three distant landmark obelisks and the Porta Pia. The intersection of Via Felice (now Via delle Quattro Fontane) and Via Pia (now Via XX Settembre) provided a fundamental boost to the further urbanization of the papal city on the eastern hillsides. Here, the canted corners of the new *quadrivium* were graced with four late sixteenth-century fountains, each one set in a niche adorned with a reclining statue.

At the south corner of the intersection, against the church of San Carlo alle Quattro Fontane, Borromini's masterpiece, a statue evidently portraying the Tiber river-god steadies a cornucopia against his left shoulder, and rests his right hand on a receptacle from which issues a steady rivulet of water; nearby a wolf looks out from behind the stalactites occluding a grotto entrance. The niche on the opposite corner houses a personification of Diana (to judge from the moon symbol in her hair), though it may represent Fidelity.

In the east corner of the intersection a male statue reclines in front of a background of bulrushes; the presence of a lion, one of the symbols of the city of Florence, would suggest a representation of the Arno. On the opposite corner of the intersection stands the niche with a recumbent female figure leaning on a lion, with a peacock at her feet; in this case the water issues from the lion's mouth. The deity represented may be Juno, or Strength (the statue is reckoned to date from 1588–93, and was restored 1990–91.

It seems that the four fountains were created upon the specific request of Sixtus V. To express his gratitude to those who completed the sculptures, in 1588 he donated four *once* of water to Muzio Mattei, the owner of a house in the block comprising the present Palazzo del Drago. In 1589 the pontiff engaged Domenico Fontana to supply five pieces of finest peperino to Muzio Mattei for the fountains at the corners of Via Felice and Via Pia, giving him permission to cannibalize material from the Septizonium (that is, the *castellum aquae* erected by Septimius Severus on the south corner of the Palatine). Sixtus' contribution is commemorated by the symbolic presence of three mounds (emblems of the papal escutcheon) set in the foreground below the figure representing Diana (or Fidelity). In 1593 his successor, the pious Florentine Clement VIII (r. 1592–1605) accorded one and a half *once* of water to Giacomo Gridenzoni for having sculpted the last of the four fountain statues.

Taken separately, the four fountains are not of any great artistic merit, though some historians attribute to the fountain on the corner of Palazzo Barberini to Pietro Berrettini da Cortona, and the other three to Domenico Fontana. What matters is the overall effect, and the scene is undoubtedly stolen by the breathtaking panoramic views of the city from the *quadrivium* requested by Pope Sixtus (whose given name Felice in Italian means both "happy" and "successful").

The Four Fountains intersection: the Arno (or Aniene) and the Tiber, respectively at the east and south corners.

Opposite
The Four Fountains intersection: the fountain of Diana (or Fidelity) on the north corner.

THE VILLA FOUNTAINS

From the sixteenth through the nineteenth centuries, under the popes the city of Rome witnessed a veritable triumph of both water and greenery. The still young metropolis (housing between 50,000 and 220,000 souls) luxuriated in a sea of vegetation. It was a city of orchards and vegetable gardens, vineyards, pastures, tillage and untended grassland, studded with magnificent town-houses and villas boasting great swathes of woodland and gardens graced with statues and many, many fountains.

For centuries these urban mansions and country estates (which were the pride of the papal and cardinalitial families) offered incomparable repositories of statuary, paintings, and countless examples of the so-called minor arts, arranged throughout the property both inside and out. To a degree, these abodes were a kind of *refugium peccatorum* for sculpture groups or statues of second rank, which often served to adorn the main fountain or fountains. The grounds of the large villas were an ideal setting for fountains of every kind, including the delightful *nymphaea* or water-gardens, affording welcome respite during the long and torrid summers of Rome.

In the pictures that follow, the photographer's lens has aptly caught the beauty of Villa Madama, Villa Giulia, the Quirinal Palace, the Vatican, Villa Medici, the Pincio gardens and Villa Borghese, Villa Aldobrandini, and Villa Doria Pamphilj. These remarkable places were each conceived as *locus amoenus*, gradually pieced together through the strategic purchase of adjacent properties. The photographs cover the many fountains, grouped according to villa.

VILLA MADAMA

Villa Madama marked the comeback of the Roman *villa suburbana*. The site commands a sweeping view of the whole of Rome, and afforded medieval pilgrims arriving from the ancient Via Cassia or Francigena their first breathtaking glimpse of the Holy City. The villa itself was designed by Raphael for Cardinal Giulio de' Medici in 1517. After the artist's death in 1520 the project passed into the hands of Giovan Francesco and Antonio da Sangallo the Younger, and Giulio Romano, who had been responsible for the interior decoration from the outset. Work had not been long under way when Rome was put to the sack in 1527 by the troops of Charles V, bringing an abrupt halt to all further progress. The new complex was planned with a fine suite of gardens, some of which were actually realized as late as the twentieth century, including a hanging garden overlooking a fish pond. Water was a primary feature of the villa and its grounds, and was used throughout in a spectacular fashion. The Elephant fountain (a portrait of the Carthaginian general Hanno, a gift to Pope Leo X from the king of Portugal) is couched in a small mosaic-filled grotto that served as a cool chamber in which to retire on a hot day.

The elaborate gilded stuccowork of the coved niche framing the Organ fountain in the Quirinal Palace gardens.

The curious Elephant fountain at Villa Madama.

The nymphaeum at Villa Giulia.

*Detail of the ornate coved vault
of the Organ fountain at the Qurinal;
a view from the bottom of the steps.*

On this page
The Venus fountain in the Quirinal
Palace gardens.

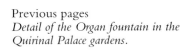

Previous pages
Detail of the Organ fountain in the
Quirinal Palace gardens.

VILLA GIULIA

Today, the two new streets of Via delle Belle Arti (opened in 1911) and Viale Tiziano impede a proper understanding of what the area north of Via Flaminia was originally like. The grounds of the villa built by Pope Julius III encompass the little oval church known as the Tempietto di Sant'Andrea and the Casino di Pio IV, describing a large area around the main building, which the pope had built in a quarter called the "Vigna Vecchia" (old vineyard). Construction work on the building commenced in 1551, and among Vignola's collaborators were Giorgio Vasari, Michelangelo, and Bartolomeo Ammannati – representing the *summa* of the finest Mannerist artists from Rome and Florence. The building's geometry is organized around a series of visual axes that depart from the atrium and end at the *nymphaeum* or water-garden, beyond the so-called Banchetti rooms, the Ionic semi-circular colonnade of the first courtyard, Ammannati's loggia, and the inner courtyard via two flights of steps that curve down into the *nymphaeum*.

Bartolomeo Ammannati built the *nymphaeum* in 1552–53. The complex three-story design was an ingenious device by which the lower story was made level with the Aqua Virgo aqueduct, making it possible to build the water-garden itself on a lower level and ensure an adequate water-pressure for the fountain. In the original scheme (which was repeatedly transformed, especially in the 1900s), the *nymphaeum* was an alluring, secluded space concealed in the heart of the villa complex.

The original grounds were more extensive, and Julius III's plan comprised a second fountain in Via Flaminia, which was built in 1552–54 by Ammannati. The new *mostra d'acque* was composed of a single Corinthian order of peperino columns and pilasters terminating in four *acroteria*; the composition abutted onto a rear colonnade rather than a true building.

Under Pius IV (r. 1559–65) the fountain was enlarged and set into a small building that encloses it. At this stage a second Ionic order was added, made of brick. Before he died, Pius donated the little building to his nephew, Carlo Borromeo, who subsequently transmitted it to his sister; it formed part of her dowry when she married Fabrizio Colonna. The Colonna family embellished the fountain with their escutcheon, adding a mascaron instead of the head of Apollo, and two dolphins on either side.

In the late 1800s the fountain had become very dilapidated, and it was not until after World War II that the municipal council effected repairs. The restoration program also included the nearby sixteenth-century fountain, whose original design included an oval basin recouped from a thermal bath. Carlo Borromeo had added a mascaron water-spout, and an architectural setting. In 1877 the fountain was restored, using the basin from the so-called Fontana del Babuino (demolished and recently rebuilt outside Sant'Atanasio).

In 1930–33 a new building was erected behind the fountain, the Cassa del Notariato, to designs by Arnaldo Foschini, who drew inspiration from the Casino di Pio IV. At this point Borromeo's architectural surround was demolished and a new fountain, the Fontana delle Conche (1934), was built in the place of the drinking trough. The basin was returned to its former home at the Fontana del Babuino.

THE QUIRINAL PALACE GARDENS

In the early 1500s the future Quirinal Palace was built as a *locus amoenus* and summer residence for the papacy, as testified by the extensive gardens behind it, which, happily, survived the sweeping urban transformations of the sixteenth and seventeenth centuries. The palace grounds vaunt numerous fountains, two of which are illustrated here.

THE FONTANA DELL'ORGANO

This rather unusual variation on the *nymphaeum* concept was commissioned by Pope Clement VIII in 1596. A grandiose architectural setting echoing the antique model of the apsed thermal hall is enhanced with stairs, balustrades, large *kantharos*-style vases, statues, mosaics, stuccoes, frescoes, and *spolveri*. At the center of the apse an artificial grotto harbors a hydraulic organ. Over the years, the fountain has regrettably been stripped of its statuary, including the figure of Apollo.

THE FONTANA DI VENERE

At the end of the 1800s the gardens stretching before the eighteenth-century coffee house of Ferdinando Fuga were graced with a new fountain designed by Giulio Monteverde. From a circular pool an irregular crag of rock serves as a base for a sculpture group (Venus bathing, with two attendants) carved by Tommaso Solari in the second half of the eighteenth century for the Reggia at Caserta. In the case of the coffee house, the "ballerina" phenomenon affecting many of Rome's fountains was applied to furniture (pictures, tapestries, statues, fountains, etc.), which made its way from one palace to another.

THE VATICAN

After the definitive return of the papacy and the Curia to Rome, attempts were made to resolve the age-old bipolarity between the Lateran and the Vatican, and the latter was declared the official seat of the successors to the Apostle. Hence, in the area adjacent to New Saint Peter's, work was resumed on the stratification of the complex of papal palaces, courtyards, and gardens. The gardens themselves were made good and in cases enlarged, as they were considered an intrinsic part of the residence of power, along with the fountains. As before, the photographer has chosen two of the many fountains in the Vatican compound.

THE FONTANA DELLA PIGNA

The Pine-cone fountain stands in the earliest part of the magnificent Belvedere Court, which was divided into three tiered sections by two successive building projects. The gardens were originally designed as a preamble to the Vatican gardens proper.

In 1608 Bramante's remarkable three-story exedra at the top of the court was transformed by Pirro Ligorio into a gargantuan niche dominated by a massive bronze *pigna* or pine-cone, and two bronze peacocks – a composition that had formerly adorned the celebrated fountain of the "Paradise" or *quadriporticus* in Constantine's basilica.

This fountain is an eye-catching feature, and has undergone several modifications over time. The pine-cone rests on an antique ornamental capital sculpted with heroic figures, and is flanked by the peacocks, whose bases rest on twin, truncated pillars; on the wall supporting the composition, an ornate mask spouts water into a semicircular basin.

THE FONTANA DEL CASINO

The Casino, meaning "small house," was built upon the express wish of the Medici pope, Pius IV (r. 1559–65), who desired a retreat immersed in the sylvan setting of the Vatican gardens. In front of the portico in the retreat's inner court, the architects Giacomo da Casignola and Giovanni da Sant'Agata installed a new fountain composed of an elegantly profiled, slightly elongated basin supported by ornamental pillars; two putti astride dolphins spout water from the rim of the basin on either side.

Details from the Pine-cone fountain in the upper court of the Belvedere.

VILLA MEDICI

In 1576 the future grand duke of Tuscany, Cardinal Ferdinando de' Medici, purchased an ancient granite fountain basin from the friars of San Salvatore in Lauro, and had it fetched to his garden at Trinità dei Monte, where it was set up in front of the villa. The

Left, and above
The mascaron water-spout from the Pine-cone fountain; one of the couchant lions.

Below
A putto riding a dolphin on the fountain at the Casino in the Vatican Gardens.

Opposite
The huge exedra of the Belvedere court framing the Pine-cone and peacocks.

PIVS · IIII · PONTIFEX · OPTIMVS · MAXIMVS ·

Florentine architect Annibale Lippi thereafter used the handsome basin to construct a fountain in one of the house's celebrated terraces, from which it was customary to admire the Roman sunsets.

THE FOUNTAIN ON THE TERRACE OF TRINITÀ DEI MONTI

In 1587 Ferdinando de' Medici purchased a broad oval granite basin of antique manufacture from the friars of San Salvatore in Lauro and had it carted to Trinità dei Monti and set up in the front garden, at the entrance to his villa. Annibale Lippi used the basin to create one of Rome's finest fountains, in a site that affords an incomparable view of the sunsets over the city.

THE FONTANA DEL MERCURIO

At the center of the entrance to the villa stands a statue of Mercury, the god of thieves and tradesmen, a copy of Giambologna's fine sculpture in Florence (1560). Mercury is seen "dancing" in the center of a circular basin supported by an ornate circular pedestal.

THE FONTANA DELL'OBELISCO

The centerpiece of this raised circular basin adorned with dolphins is a copy of the Egyptian obelisk discovered in the Temple of Isis near the church of Santa Maria sopra Minerva. In 1788 the successors to the Medici, the Lorena, had the original obelisk taken to Florence, to beautify the famous Boboli Gardens above Palazzo Pitti.

THE FOUNTAIN OF THE NYMPHAEUM

In actual fact, this is an outdoor *nymphaeum*, containing three statues set into niches (two rectangular, and one apsidal); below the central statue a mascaron disgorges a steady flow of water into an ancient sarcophagus.

THE PINCIO

In early antiquity this hill was decked with fine examples of the Roman *hortus* or urban garden. In the sixteenth century the land was involved in the construction of the Villa Medici, but the summit itself – which offers a superb view across the city – was still unspoiled. At the turn of the eighteenth century, therefore, the architect who masterminded the redesign of the Piazza del Popolo below, Giuseppe Valadier, remodeled the hilltop as a *passeggiata* or pastoral walk that also provided a gorgeous verdant backdrop for the square. With its flights of steps, terracing, and gardens, the Pincio became one of the favorite haunts of Pope Pius IX during the spring and summer months. In the late nineteenth and early twentieth centuries, the period of the Third Rome, the Pincio and the Corso (Via del Corso) were enhanced to accommodate the steady procession of elegant horses and carriages owned by the wealthy upper classes, who thereby strove to emulate the nobility and provided a colorful parade for the benefit of their less privileged onlookers. To this purpose, in 1908 an overpass was built across the Muro Torto (a stretch of ancient fortified walling) to provide direct access from the Pincio gardens to the grounds of the nearby Villa Borghese.

At the top of the richly planted zigzagging road climbing the Pincio hill in Piazza Napoleone stands one of the so-called "ballerina" or "traveling" fountains, but the photographer has also captured two otherwise hidden jewels of the gardens.

Villa Medici: the Mercury fountain, and the Obelisk fountain.

THE WATER CLOCK

A rocky crag emerging from a small pond shoulders an elegant glazed tower containing a fascinating water clock designed by the Dominican monk Giambattista Embriaco in 1872, a work of great ingenuity that has been sadly left to fall into disrepair.

Opposite
The little fountain on the terrace of the delightful Casino, built by Pirro Ligorio for Pope Pius IV, in the Vatican Gardens.

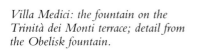

Villa Medici: the fountain on the Trinità dei Monti terrace; detail from the Obelisk fountain.

Opposite
Close-up of the central element of the fountain on the Trinità dei Monti terrace.

The Pincio: the Water Clock fountain, and the Amphora fountain.

Opposite
Villa Medici: the Nymphaeum fountain, with its three niches and statues.

Villa Borghese: one of the figures from the Lions fountain, and a jocose waterspout in the Giardino del Lago.

Opposite
Villa Borghese: detail from the Sea Horses fountain.

THE FONTANA DELL'ANFORA

In a circular pool near the Casina Valadier a boulder supports a bronze statue of a nymph filling an *amphora* with water, the work of Amleto Cataldi (1912).

VILLA BORGHESE

At the beginning of the seventeenth century Cardinal Scipione Borghese, the favorite nephew of Pope Paul V, commissioned from Flaminio Ponzio the redevelopment of a large tract of land immediately outside the Porta del Popolo. The request was for a rambling Renaissance-style park (divided into three parts, a spinney, a landscaped garden with architectural settings and statues, and a more untended rustic area); a handsome *casino* was erected in the grounds to house the family collections of art works, together with a small theater and an aviary.

Without delay, Giovanni Fontana constructed a small aqueduct to carry running water from the Acqua Vergine to the buildings and the numerous fountains envisaged by Ponzio's project. After the latter's death work continued under the supervision of Giovanni Vasanzio (the Flemish architect Jan van Santen), who was succeeded by Girolamo Rainaldi.

In the second half of the eighteenth century the Borghese heir Marcantonio commissioned Antonio Asprucci to enlarge the villa and gardens (which eventually covered an area of some seventy-eight hectares), by building anew or renovating existing structures and architectural backdrops, reworking the Renaissance gardens in the new Romantic style (with sham ruins and other follies) imported from England. Naturally, Asprucci's brief included reinstating the park's fountains.

The new layout was developed further in the course of the nineteenth and twentieth centuries, when the Villa Borghese gardens became the property of the municipal council (1901), and was subsequently linked up to the Pincio gardens. In the 1920s and 1930s the architect Raffaele de Vico built a service reservoir to ensure the supply of water to the various ponds and fountains (both ancient and recent, original or modified) scattered through this immense parkland.

THE FONTANA DEI CAVALLI MARINI

The fountain, named after the four rearing sea horses of the centerpiece, was designed by Luigi Salimeni and Cristoforo Unterberger (1790–91) as part of the enlargement scheme of the Villa Borghese gardens supervised by Antonio and Mario Asprucci. In a circular *pelagos*, or pool, four equine *chimerae* bear aloft a broad circular basin surmounted by two bowls of diminishing sizes, from the uppermost of which flows an abundant stream of water that cascades down each level of the composition.

THE FONTANE DEI LEONI

In the early nineteenth century, alongside the Lion Portico (an architectural backdrop of considerable beauty built by the Asprucci) Luigi Canina installed these fountains, with their Egyptian lions discharging jets of water.

THE FONTANA DEL MOSÈ SALVATO

The work of the sculptor Di Brazzà, the "Moses in the Bulrushes" fountain comprises a circular pool inset with an island of bulrushes with the basket in which the baby Moses was rescued from the water by the pharaoh's daughter; on either side rises a jet of water.

THE FONTANA DEL TEMPIETTO NEL GIARDINO DEL LAGO

During the extensive remodeling of the gardens at the end of the eighteenth century, an area of the Villa Borghese grounds was set aside for a Lake Garden. Here, on an island

Villa Borghese: the Lions fountain, and the delightful Tempietto in the Giardino del Lago.

Opposite
Villa Borghese: the Sea Horses fountain.

Villa Borghese: the Moses in the Bulrushes fountain.

in the middle of the pond, stands a small Ionic temple (Asprucci, 1785–87) housing a robed statue of the god of medicine, Aesculapius. Completing the arrangement are nymphs and bas-reliefs, neatly encapsulating the neoclassical mood of the period.

VILLA DORIA PAMPHILJ

In 1630 Pamphilio Pamphilj purchased a vineyard outside the Walls of Aurelian, and in 1640–44 the family bought up a further twenty-three vineyards, thereby greatly enlarging their estate, upon which they proceeded to construct a casino with annexes as soon as Cardinal Pamphilj was elected to the papal throne in 1644, as Innocent X.

In the decades that followed, the family, now known by the name of Doria Landi Pamphilj, continued building on their property, expanding into the surrounding land. By 1850, with the acquisition of the adjacent Villa Corsini alle Quattro Venti, the Pamphilj estate had grown to some 180 hectares, graced with fine buildings and countless statues, fountains, and ponds.

Among the park's many fountains, one in particular has a somewhat spotted history, the Fontana della Lumaca or Snail fountain. At an earlier date, Bernini had commissioned from Angelo Vannellini a complex sculpture group for the Fontana del Moro in Piazza Navona; the composition involved a large shell held up by the tails of three dolphins. When it was unveiled in May 1652 the patron was unimpressed, and the locals rather disparagingly dubbed it "The Snail." The pope passed it on to his sister, Olimpia Pamphilj, who had it installed in the gardens (no longer extant) at Ripa, near Santa Maria in Cappella. In the eighteenth century the group was relocated to Villa Doria Pamphilj and incorporated into the so-called Snail fountain. Actually the group in the garden fountain is a copy, and the original is in the Museo di Palazzo Doria Pamphilj.

Throughout the eighteenth and nineteenth centuries the Pamphilj family continued to embellish their retreat with new buildings, sepulchers, residences, and pavilions for entertaining guests. Many of the new fountains they created were styled on those of antiquity or after some fantastic design, such as the Cupid fountain, or the Waterfall Nymphaeum. Today, as with the buildings, the fountains are in a ruinous state, and the pond is overrun with water-rats.

Opposite
Villa Doria Pamphilj: the central element of the so-called Snail fountain.

Following pages
Front prospect of Villa Doria Pamphilj; the Lily fountain.

Villa Doria Pamphilj: view of the so-called Snail fountain; close-up of the moss-encrusted Lily fountain.

Opposite
Villa Doria Pamphilj: view of the Cupid fountain.

THE "BALLERINA" FOUNTAINS

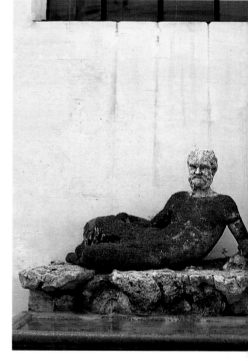

The peculiar reclining silenus figure of the so-called Babuino or "Simpleton" fountain.

Ever since the times of Constantine the Great, whose monumental arch is a signal reminder of his grandeur and renown, the Romans and their patrons had frequent recourse to cannibalizing ancient monuments for new developments and constructions, using their materials either to rehabilitate existing monuments, or to construct new ones. Statues, bas-reliefs, columns, capitals, and the like found their way into the fabric of other buildings.

This habit of reusing materials from earlier epochs escalated in the Christian city and the ensuing papal Rome, when the vestiges of the past provided a ready source of superb stone and ornamental details. For centuries the cardinals and pontiffs plundered the ruins of imperial Rome, even appropriating obelisks and other landmarks, big or small. In the specific field of fountains, Bernini put a small obelisk to new use for his Fontana dei Fiumi in Piazza Navona. An obelisk was likewise employed as the crowning feature for the Pantheon fountain. Recycling became so universally accepted that even such architects as Borromini (who should have known better) canvassed his patrons for permission to transform the eye-catching pyramid of the wealthy *praetor* Caius Cestius (set in the Aurelian Wall near Porta San Paolo) into a church dedicated to Saints Peter and Paul.

In fact, much of the materials used for the fountains of Rome were recouped from some earlier monument or other; prime examples include the lions in the fountain at the foot of the Capitol's graded ramp, and those originally stationed at either side of the Pantheon fountain (which were later removed upon the behest of Sixtus V to adorn the new terminus for his Acqua Felice). Similarly, the obelisk and titanic statues of Castor and Pollux commanding the square outside the Quirinal Palace were also appropriated from an earlier setting.

This recycled material included components of every kind, including statuary, such as the figure of Marforio which Giacomo Della Porta inserted into the fountain on the Capitoline Hill. But the most frequently reused items were the huge marble or granite basins of imperial manufacture, which so conveniently suited the purpose of fountain construction. A prime example can be seen in the Fontana del Babuino (later resited in Via Flaminia, and only recently reunited with the so-called "babuino" or *silenus* figure). Another such case is the vast granite bowl (found alongside the Arch of Septimius Severus), which Della Porta used for the fountain in the Campo Vaccino. The basin later became a sunken pool due to the raising of the ground level, but reemerged in the early 1800s when it was disinterred by Carlo Fea. In 1818 Raffaele Stern was engaged by Pius VII to reuse the basin and marble balustrade enclosure for the new fountain being installed outside the Quirinal Palace.

Another basin from the imperial period was purchased for 200 *scudi* by Cardinal Ferdinando de' Medici and amalgamated with other elements for the fountain in the forecourt of his villa between the Pincio and Trinità dei Monti; likewise, Alexander VI resited an ancient imperial tub as a drinking trough complementing the first fountain that stood in Saint Peter's Square; this was later removed by Alexander VII.

Opposite
Spouting chimaera from the Acqua Paola fountain in Piazza Trilussa.

Among the numerous basins of antiquity reused in papal Rome, one of the most curious cases is the rectangular tub of granite unearthed in 1579 in Via dei Leutari and promptly relocated (as ever, by Giacomo Della Porta) in the center of Piazza Navona, raised on a low plinth, with columns and a railing. Some decades later, Gianlorenzo Bernini cleared everything away to make way for the Fontana dei Fiumi; in 1650 the rectangular basin was shifted to a new position toward its counterpart at the north end of Piazza Navona; and finally, in 1870 it was transferred to the Villa Borghese gardens and set up in the Giardino del Lago. Here it is encircled by a sunken pool and adorned with masks and tritons (transposed from the Fontana del Moro in Piazza Navona), thereby assuming the name of the Fontana delle Maschere, or Masks fountain.

Still on the subject of the retrieval and reuse of carved stone basins from ancient Rome, another extraordinary case is the antique porphyry tub which the indefatigable Della Porta borrowed for his Fontana del Pantheon: after the fountain was remodeled in 1740, the basin was taken to the church of San Giovanni in Laterano, where it was somewhat improperly used as the sarcophagus of Clement XII.

In essence, it had become standard practice throughout Rome to reuse entire fountains or pieces of them to create new ones. Tradition, however, is never as enduring and immovable as it may seem, as it is invariably the end result of a gradual stratification of successive innovations.

The vestiges of ancient Rome were not the only source of recyclable materials for new fountains, however. Even architectural fountains of more recent date were pillaged for what they could provide for new installations. The mascaron or mask feature which Giacomo Della Porta had contracted out for his hapless fountain in Campo Vaccino (1596) was evidently used twice over. When the latter fountain was dismantled in 1827 the mascaron was transferred to the fountain at the Porto Leonino on the right bank of the Tiber, opposite San Giovanni de' Fiorentini. In 1890 this fountain was demolished, too, to make way for the high walls that embank the river. Thus, in 1936 Della Porta's mask made its way to the fountain in the square of San Pietro d'Illiria on the Aventine.

A similar fate befell the round, eighteenth-century fountain in the Casino Borghese, with its statue of Venus, which replaced an earlier design by Vasanzio, known as the Fontana del Narciso; at the end of the eighteenth century the basin of this composition was reused for the Fontana dei Pupazzi in the east sector of the Villa Borghese gardens.

Another case, perhaps slightly more convoluted, concerns several components of one of the fountains in Piazza del Popolo, designed and built by Giacomo Della Porta in 1572. The monument was demolished by Giuseppe Valadier at the end of the eighteenth century; in 1823 it made its way to the church of San Pietro in Montorio, whence it was removed in 1940 to the municipal storerooms and partially restored (and modified), only to turn up again in Piazza Nicosia in 1950. However, the tritons that once adorned Della Porta's fountains in the early 1800s are now at the Fontana del Moro in Piazza Navona; here they were restored in 1813. In 1873 copies were made by Luigi Amici, and – to complicate matters further – these copies are now the ones in Piazza Navona, while the originals are in the Villa Borghese, in the Giardino del Lago.

Another example: in Viale Goethe, which cuts across the southwest corner of the villa gardens, an antique sarcophagus serves as a base for one of the four marble sculpture groups that Della Porta had envisaged for *his* fountain at the Pantheon.

It should be said that the practice of recycling pieces from antique fountains was just as common this century, both during the radical transformation of the city between the wars, and in the 1950s and 1960s. As noted in the Foreword, the phenomenon deserves discussing in more detail. One such example is offered by the large drinking trough that once flanked the fountain outside the church of Santa Maria in Cosmedin, the Fontana dei Tritoni (Piazza di Bocca della Verità). After several clearance schemes in the area, which created a desert in place of an incomparable agglomeration of some thousand years of history (the Cloaca Maxima, and the kilns of the industrial neighborhood alongside the Circus Maximus), the drinking-trough was moved to the Lungotevere, where it is scarcely visible alongside the rushing traffic.

The fountains of Piazza Nicosia and Piazza San Simeone.

For this section of the book, the photographer Francesco Venturi has grouped together eight fountains that have each in their way earned the appellation "ballerina" for their repeated relocations from one part of the city to the other, thereby underscoring just how frequent and widespread was the custom of reusing – either partially or entirely – the material and elements of the fountains of antiquity.

The eight examples here are shown in chronological order, according to their foundation date: the fountain in Piazza Nicosia (1572), the Fontana del Babuino (1576), the fountain in Piazza San Simeone (1589), the Fontana della Terrina (1590), the fountain in Piazza Sant'Andrea della Valle (Ponte Paolo V), the fountain of the Acqua Paola in Piazza Trilussa (1613), the Fontana delle Api (1644), the fountain at the Ripetta river port (1708).

THE FOUNTAIN IN PIAZZA NICOSIA

Originally sited in Piazza del Popolo, the fountain was part of a group designed by Giacomo Della Porta as part of a redevelopment program (ratified in 1570) for the utilization and distribution of water from the newly augmented Aqua Virgo system. The two models on which the architect largely based his designs were the first fountain erected in Saint Peter's Square, and that of Santa Maria in Trastevere.

In 1572 Della Porta apprised Cardinal Ricci of his project for the reworking of Piazza del Popolo (borrowing the Trastevere fountain's motif of an octagonal basin with superimposed bowls). Ricci therewith commissioned the task from the sculptor Giovanni Leminard (perhaps of French origin), and supplied him with marble blocks that had been found on the slopes of the Quirinal, requesting him to have the basin ready within a few months. In October 1572 a few unassuming ornamental features were provided for the new fountain, which was inaugurated early the following year.

The resulting composition, at once branded as inept, was dwarfed by the emptiness of the vast and rather neglected square. At this, a new commission was issued for four tritons. The artists engaged were a certain Simone (called Moschino), Taddeo Landini, Cristoforo Fiammingo, and Giacomo Silla Longhi. But the four statues turned out to be ungainly, and were redirected to the Fontana del Moro (another of Della Porta's designs) in Piazza Navona.

In 1575 the height of the fountain's plinth was reduced, as the delivery capacity was too weak to ensure a decent jet of water. Much later, in the early eighteenth century, further alterations were made to the fountain, with the addition of four dragons and four eagles (symbols from the Borghese coat of arms).

When it came for Giuseppe Valadier to restructure Piazza del Popolo, the fountain was judged to be too unassuming, and in 1823 it was duly transferred to the Janiculum, outside the church of San Pietro in Montorio. But its travels were not over.

Around 1940 the fountain was removed from its new site and restored; the basin and balustered enclosure were changed, while the emblems of Gregory XIII (r. 1572–85) were supplanted with those of the Borghese in honor of the city governor during the Fascist period, Gian Giacomo Borghese. The "ballerina" fountain was temporarily stored in the municipal repository, not to reemerge until 1950, when it was transported to Piazza Nicosia. As it stands today, the only genuine part from the original fountain is the octagonal basin, the rest of its features are either copies or details added later.

THE FONTANA DEL BABUINO

In 1576 Alessandro Grandi adorned the facade of his family residence in Via del Babuino with an ancient square vase sculpted from a piece of African marble, and added the statue that earned the nickname of the "babuino," meaning simpleton.

The said figure was probably meant to represent a *silenus*, or was a copy of an ancient portrait of Semo Sancus, a half-goat, half-human Sabine deity. At any event, owing to

The ancient fountain formerly in Piazza Scossacavalli, reassembled outside Sant'Andrea della Valle.

Opposite
The characteristic Tureen fountain outside the Chiesa Nuova.

its striking ugliness, the figure soon lent its name to the street itself, which was previously known as Via Paolina Trifaria.

In 1584 repairs were made to the wall fountain and it assumed an indeterminately Renaissance tone, as can be seen from a rather sketchy portrait by Domenico Parasacchi. In 1738 the Boncompagni bought the residence and decided to enclose the basin in a handsome architectural *mostra d'acqua*, framed by rusticated pilasters that delimit the section over the water, from which emerge two superimposed dolphins (the family emblem).

The statue from which the fountain (and street) took its name was set into a niche within the *mostra*, and was raised upon a fictive rocky protrusion which discharged the water that filled the tub below.

At the time the *silenus* was still intact. An eye-witness description dated 1756–57 records that the figure was seen, moreover, to be holding a *zampogna* or wind instrument. By 1838, however, both hands were missing, as testified by Antonio Nibby; and a later drawing by Giovan Battista Giovenale, dating from after 1870, shows a mutilated statue with a wineskin on his knee, from which the fountain's water splashes into the tub below.

The year 1877 saw improvements to the drains and the sidewalk outside what would become Palazzo Cerasi: the fountain had to be temporarily moved, and the *silenus*, or god Sancus, together with his rocky throne, was relegated to a corner of the courtyard; the basin, meanwhile, was used as a drinking trough on Via Flaminia, alongside the Ammannati fountain.

In 1925 a proposal was made to combine the basin and the fountain in Via del Babuino in a new site just to the left of the church of Sant'Atanasio. In 1934 the drinking trough on Via Flaminia made way for a fountain, the Fontana delle Conche, but the trough was not reunited with its former composition.

Later, after the war, a group of local residents managed to obtain the municipality's pledge to restore the fountain to its original state. In 1957 the statue and basin were bequeathed to the local council. In order to reconstitute the two components, the *silenus* was cleaned and his left arm was bolted to what was left of his rocky seat; the group was then set up behind the tub, and the entire composition raised upon a step.

THE FOUNTAIN IN PIAZZA SAN SIMEONE

This fountain originally resided in 1589 in Piazza Montanara, and was built to designs by Giacomo Della Porta. The project envisaged a square base with a low plinth supporting a round travertine basin embellished with four coats of arms; at its the center a small square stand supported a little railing of the top basin, together with four sculpted mascarons that discharged the water into the tub below. Both this and the main tub were the work of Pietro Gucci. Eight twin colonettes, without a railing, encircled the composition, which was sited in the higher part of the piazza.

The original fountain underwent several alterations over time, most notably in 1696 and 1829. Eventually it was removed (1932) when urban developments summarily erased the piazza from the map in the course of a major clearance scheme in the Capitol area. The fountain's first stopover was in the Giardino degli Aranci on the Aventine; it was transferred to its present site in Piazza San Simeone in 1973.

THE FONTANA DELLA TERRINA AT CHIESA NUOVA

The original design for this fountain is once again attributable to Giacomo Della Porta, and was intended for Campo de' Fiori (see relevant section), one of the vital hubs of Renaissance and Baroque Rome. Built in 1590, the fountain at first comprised a sculpted marble basin set into a pool, both oval; in 1621 the basin was given a travertine lid, making it resemble a soup tureen, whence its popular name.

The Acqua Paola fountain in Piazza Trilussa.

In 1889 a new monument to the sixteenth-century philosopher Giordano Bruno was erected in the Campo, and the fountain was removed to the municipal storerooms (1892).

In the upheavals that followed papal Rome's transition to being the capital of the newly declared Kingdom of Italy, the narrow *piazzetta* of the Chiesa Nuova – dominated by the facade of the oratory of the Order of Saint Philip Neri, ingeniously designed by Borromini to conform with the square's cramped conditions – was further reduced, subordinating its role to that of a brief clearing in the new thoroughfare of Corso Vittorio Emanuele II (named after the first sovereign of united Italy). In 1924 the square welcomed the Fontana della Terrina, which was installed in a sunken rectangular pool. Today the fountain has a forlorn, neglected appearance and its pool is usually cluttered with refuse of all kinds.

The Fountain at Sant'Andrea della Valle

This fountain was originally erected in Piazza di Scossacavalli, between Palazzo Penitenzieri, Palazzo Torlonia, Palazzo dei Convertendi, and the church of San Giacomo Scossacavalli. Its design is traditionally attributed to Carlo Maderno, who was at the time involved in remodeling the fountain of Saint Peter's Square.

The capacious travertine basin was raised on two high steps, also in travertine. A jet of water rose at each of the four sides of the basin. The centerpiece was a round bowl on a square cippus bearing the eagle and dragon emblems of the Borghese, with the escutcheon of Paul V. The upper bowl was adorned with a sort of aquatic plant that spouted the central jet of water. The fountain's enclosure consisted of sixteen low bollards or posts, mostly in granite, joined by a solid iron rail.

The demolition of the so-called Spina in the Borgo ward during urban renewal operations in 1937 threatened the fountain's permanence, but it was not removed. In fact, in October 1941 it was still in place, though some pieces had been dismantled and stored out of harm's way behind a fence.

In March 1944, during the German occupation, the components were taken to a municipal storeroom on the Lungotevere Aventino. The remains of the fountain were definitively demolished in January 1945.

Subsequently, the municipal authorities favored the fountain's reconstruction in Piazza della Pilotta, where there was scheme to complete the square's urban furniture. The dismantled pieces were therefore parked on a nearby lawn in the garden of Cardinal Bessarione, and a hasty attempt made to reassemble the fountain, at which point it became evident that the upper bowl was missing. Rumors of a scheme for an underground carport in Piazza della Pilotta further complicated matters, and the fountain's resurrection was deferred.

In 1955 the municipality began to look around for a new site for what remained of the monument. Finally, in 1959 the former Scossacavalli fountain was reconstituted with a new bowl (in concrete), and became a traffic island, albeit an artistic one.

The Acqua Paola fountain in Piazza Trilussa

This *mostra terminale* for the Acqua Paola aqueduct (known fondly as the "Fontanone") was originally sited in the Regola district on the left bank of the Tiber, and was set into the wall of the San Sisto hospice at Ponte Sisto.

The original fountain was built in 1613 by Giovanni Fontana and the Flemish architect Jan van Sant (who adopted the Italian name of Giovanni Vasanzio), and consisted of a deep niche flanked by two spouting dragons (the Borghese family emblems). The water supply was not intended solely for the hospice's use, but served the entire borough via two conduits, one of which terminated in Piazza Giuda, and other in Via Giulia, near Palazzo Sacchetti.

The Bees fountain in Piazza Barberini.

~ 142 ~

In 1844 the wall-fountain was enclosed within an iron railing anchored to six low half-columns in red granite. In 1879, when work began on the construction of the Muraglione (the walling-in of the river) and the Lungotevere embankment avenues, the fountain had to be demolished. The general uproar that ensued was carried on through the press. Despite protests, even from abroad, the clearance scheme erased both the fountain and the hospice.

In 1883 the municipality conceded rebuilding the fountain – on the right bank of the river, however. While demolition had been notoriously expeditious, the fountain's reconstruction was a long drawn-out affair, lasting years. After over a decade, the press took up the issue once more, and in 1897 the municipal authorities were compelled to resume the promised work. Alas, the original pieces of the fountain had meanwhile been dispersed; after some searching they were traced to the storerooms of the national museum annexed to the Baths of Diocletian; others turned up at the various municipal depots. Some pieces of travertine had been scattered carelessly around the grass verges of the Forte Bravetta, probably by someone who had ideas of reusing them on some other job.

Work one the fountain's reconstruction finally commenced in 1898, and it was re-assembled as a free-standing monument. The result was disappointing, and the Trastevere locals have always felt that it rather resembles a funerary vault.

THE FONTANA DELLA CONCHIGLIA (OR FONTANA DELLE API) IN PIAZZA BARBERINI

In a watercolor by Roesler Franz depicting the Fontana del Tritone (see relative section), one can make out the Fontana della Conchiglia (or delle Api) at the corner of Via Felice (now Via Sistina). Today it occupies a different site, at the corner of Via Veneto.

The original fountain was a drinking trough whose convenient shape led it to be built into the corner of a house. It was created in 1644 by Gianlorenzo Bernini and, like his nearby Fontana del Tritone, it was dedicated to his patron, Pope Urban VIII. Contrary to the intentions of the artist and the pontiff, the dedication became the butt of frequent jokes. The fan-shaped commemoration plaque stated that the fountain was made in the twenty-second year of Urban's papacy, and there is the rub: the pope had so far ruled only twenty-one years. He was accused of being unable to count, and of trying to predict the future. He was also charged with "stealing time," just as he had plundered Rome for its countless treasures. (The *pasquinade* runs: "Havendo li Berberini succhiato tutto il mondo, ora volevano anche succhiare il tempo.") To stem the tide of protest, the extra Roman numeral was chiseled out, and, as fate would have it, the Barberini pope went to meet his Maker, just eight days before entering the twenty-second year of his pontificate.

Before the redevelopment of the present-day streets of Via del Tritone, Via Barberini, and Via Veneto, the corner of Via Felice was increasingly busy and the fountain was becoming a traffic hazard. In 1867 it was therefore dismantled and put in storage, but did not see the light of day again until 1917; this time it was not attached to a wall, but set away from the building behind it (Palazzo Coppadé).

Today it is difficult to assess the fountain's original dimensions. Its current configuration comprises a large scallop, its top half open in a vertical position to expose its contents. At the join, three giant bees, arranged symmetrically, seem to be sipping at the fine jets of water that spout steadily into the lower, horizontal, valve of the shell.

The composition is not faithful to the original: the inside of the lower valve of the shell was once fluted, but is now smooth, and the words "URBIS ORNATUM" in the dedication have become "URBIS ORNAMENTUM." As for the bees, only the central one is authentic, and its companions are somewhat graceless copies. The renovation was carried out with travertine from the ancient Porta Salaria, which was demolished together with the adjacent stretch of the Aurelianic walls.

The ancient quay-side fountain of Ripetta, with its metal lantern.

THE FOUNTAIN AT RIPETTA

The riverside port known as the Ripetta was built in 1708 by Alessandro Specchi and Carlo Fontana under the supervision of Monsignor Niccolò Giudice. The port – which disappeared when the Tiber's banks were walled in and the Lungotevere constructed – served as a loading quay for supplies to the Papal State, usually consisting of foodstuffs (especially oil and wine), but also wood and building material.

Level with the church of San Rocco a broad, concave flight of steps descended to the river. A small fountain was installed during the papacy of Clement XI (r. 1700–21) in a concave clearing at the top of the steps, hard by the church. The new fountain was composed of a low travertine plinth and two basins, one above the other. At the top of the composition rose a kind of sculpted crag adorned with a scallop shell flanked by a pair of dolphins. The rocky formation culminated in a triple peak, the tallest of which was surmounted by a star, one of the emblems of the Albani family coat of arms.

The walling-in of the Tiber and the construction of the riverside streets along the new embankments entailed eliminating the port; actually, the port was covered over, whereas the fountain was dismantled and its components put into storage. Later it was entrusted to the British School, which proceeded to carry out a preliminary restoration in the hope of re-erecting it in a new site.

At the end of the 1920s the fountain was indeed reassembled in the clearing above the old Porto di Ripetta, between the Tiber and Via Ripetta. But the fountain had been tampered with and was seriously altered. Furthermore, its relocation in a completely different context, away from its port surroundings, meant the fountain had lost its original function: it had formerly doubled up as a small lighthouse, its lantern (still crowning the fountain) affording a welcome lamp guiding boats on their way down-river.

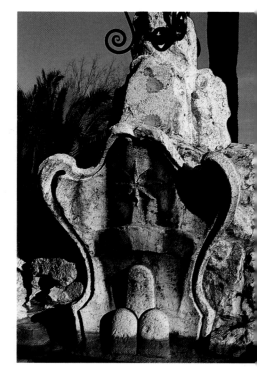

Detail of the Ripetta quay-side fountain.

THE NEIGHBORHOOD
FOUNTAINS
OF PIETRO LOMBARDI

In the second half of the 1920s the various officers and technicians under the then
governor of the city were inundated with protests from scholars of Roman history
over the indiscriminate use of a new type of fountain, composed of a cylindrical
body in cast-iron, known as "nasoni" (snouts) owing to the unendearing shape of
their water-spout.

All was not lost, however. The early years of the century saw the emergence of the
sculptor-architect Pietro Lombardi (Rome 1894–1984), one of whose early commissions was for the little fountain in Piazza Scossacavalli, a sibling of Carlo Maderno's
monumental work (see relative description for the fountain of Sant'Andrea della Valle).
Lombardi's work was summarily erased in the redevelopment of the Spina di Borgo,
and is only documented in a single photograph, taken some time after 1930.

Shortly afterward Lombardi built a larger fountain (generally considered his masterpiece), the Fontana delle Anfore (1926), originally conceived for the central square of
the Testaccio quarter and later transferred to Piazza dell'Emporio. The very name of the
square neatly epitomizes the outsize dimensions of the imperial freight yard, a vast hub
for the exchange of goods in imperial times, whose immense turnover led to the creation in three centuries of the so-called *mons testaceus*, a veritable mountain of potsherds
of discarded terra-cotta containers, particularly *amphorae*, which were used in antiquity
for transporting foodstuffs.

Built on a near-monumental scale, the fountain had a dual message: the upward
movement of the central feature with its cluster of *amphorae*, and the exclusive use of
rounded forms, making sure each corner was rounded and the joins between the various elements made smooth. For the author, the *amphora* in this case was not only a
symbol for the *rione* or ward, but served as a module for each sculptural solution, favor-
ing the downward flow of water from the top to the basin at the base.

In the meantime, Lombardi obtained a commission to construct a series of new
neighborhood fountains whose design was to bear in mind the emblems or symbols of
the dominant craft of the neighborhood in question. These fountains were inaugurated
to mark the fifth anniversary of the Marcia su Roma (the famous march of the Fascists
from the north of Italy to the capital), but, despite working directly for the city's gov-
erning corporation, Lombardi steered clear of rhetorical celebrations of the regime.
The common feature of the fountains was the inclusion of local symbols illustrating the
different types of trade or craft activity.

As a result, his work for the wards of Borgo, the Tiburtino, Sant'Eustachio, Pigna, the
Esquiline, Ripa, Trastevere, and Campus Martius, was always in tone with the long and
stratified history of each neighborhood.

It has sometimes been claimed that the fountain outside the church of Santa Croce in
Gerusalemme is also the work of Lombardi; in fact it was built (1927) by Adolfo Marini, unless Lombardi was the designer and Marini the sculptor. This has yet to be established through more in-depth research.

*The Amphorae fountain in Piazza
dell'Emporio.*

The fountain of the Monti quarter, and the Porta Castello fountain with its pyramid of canon-balls.

Right
The Pine-cone fountain in Piazza San Marco.

Opposite
The Ripa neighborhood wall-fountain at the hospice of San Michele a Ripa.

The Tiaras fountain near the colonnade of Saint Peter's.

THE FONTANELLA OF THE MONTI QUARTER

The fountain is situated in Via San Vito, near the arch of Gallienus or Porta Viminale, one of the gates serving the curtain of urban fortifications traditionally known as the Wall of Servius. The fountain embodies the symbols of three hills of the Monti quarter, the Viminal, Esquiline, and Caelian. As it happened, when Lombardi installed his fountain, this corner of the Monti quarter had become a separate ward, known as Esquilino (of which the Castro Pretorio quarter is an off-shoot); similarly, Celio was declared an independent ward in 1921. On a complex system of steps stands a trilobate base from which rises a cluster of domed cylindrical forms embellished with star-shapes, several of which serve as water-spouts, issuing into three semicircular basins that overflow into a grate in the pavement.

THE FONTANELLA OF PORTA CASTELLA IN BORGO

Just beyond the arches of the Passetto, set into the wall on the right one comes across this little fountain framed in a round arch in fine travertine stone (outlined in brick laid edgeways in a recent and somewhat unattractive renovation). A large travertine dado shoulders a cluster of cannonballs (which would appear to allude to the piles that can be seen in the upper court of the adjacent Castel Sant'Angelo), between which a faun water-spout issues a jet of water downward into a basin, whose border was once decorated with sporadic cannonballs (now lost).

THE FONTANELLA DELLA PIGNA IN PIAZZA SAN MARCO

With this fountain, Lombardi took his cue from the Pine-cone fountain in the Cortile della Pigna at the Vatican Belvedere. Hemmed in by rushing traffic, the little garden fountain is composed of a pine-cone perched on a stylized corolla-capital of flowers (probably tulips), and the water flows from several outlets into two superimposed circular basins and thence to the pool at ground level. The travertine pavement is delimited by four low pillars.

THE FONTANELLA DELLE TIARE

Situated alongside the Passetto at the end of Via di Porta Angelica, this charming work stands at the opening of the piazza of the so-called Città Leonina. In the shadow of the colonnade a low step supports a pool divided into three basins; from a circular base rises the characteristic Lombardi composite trunk, crowned by four papal tiaras (whence the fountain's name). The three lower tiaras are accompanied by the keys of Saint Peter symbolizing the dual powers of the pontiff over both spiritual and temporal matters; from the keys the water flows first into three jutting dishes and then into the pool at the bottom.

THE FONTANELLA AT RIPA

Abutting the apostolic hospice of San Michele a Ripa (now the seat of the Ministry of Cultural Heritage), the fountain overlooks the remodeled site of the ancient port of Ripa Grande, which was effectively erased with the embankment of the Tiber and the construction of the Lungotevere. The little fountain carries the Ripa symbol of two nautical-type columns framing a helm and tiller. The water issues from the center of the composition into a suspended bowl and then over a semicircular step of porphyry.

Opposite
The Artists fountain in Via Margutta.

The Barrel fountain.

THE FONTANELLA DELLA CASCATELLE

Lombardi sited this small fountain for the Tiburtino district just outside the monumental entrance to the Campo Verano cemetery. Originally the architect did not draw from the characteristics of the neighborhood, which doubled in size toward Pontonaccio during the 1920s; nor was he influenced by the cemetery. The free-standing fountain takes after the idea of the milestone, flanked by two small half-columns and surmounted by a semicircular cornice in travertine. Three mounds disgorge water into thee basins; from the last, at pavement level, the water spills out into the grate of the street drain. The fountain was destroyed in an air raid during World War II.

THE FONTANELLA DEGLI ARTISTI

Situated in Via Margutta and adorned with the tools-of-trade of this characteristic artists' quarter (easels, paintbrushes, and chisels), this wall-fountain advertises a well-known feature of the city. Since the seventeenth century, artists great and small (and also many would-be daubers) have crammed Via Margutta and the adjacent streets, living alongside the local craftsmen. The painters and sculptors were followed by hosts of photographers, film directors, antiques dealers, and curiosity shop owners. Many of the nearby rooms, once for coal men and tanners, have been accorded the high-sounding name of *garçonniere*. As with his other neighborhood fountains, Lombardi has devised an ingenious solution: the fountain is encased in a marble frame attached to the wall; the water, however, flows out of the open-mouthed mascarons and compasses into basins, before spilling out into the grate of the street drain.

THE FONTANELLA DELLA SAPIENZA

Also known as the Libri or Books fountain, Lombardi has set this composition into a square surround in Via degli Staderari in the Sapienza or university district. Given the location, the design includes a stag with a cross in its antlers (referring to the emblem on the church dedicated to the second-century Roman general, according to a legend that stems from ancient Iranian folklore); the stag's head is flanked by shelves bearing enormous folio volumes, slightly tattered from continual use by the university students. From each tome hangs a bookmark that guides the flow of water directly onto the grate of the drain in the sidewalk.

THE FONTANELLA DELLA BOTTE

Here there was no easy symbol, like the tiller for the Ripa neighborhood fountain. Since the end of the 1800s, the Trastevere quarter has been steadily losing its once highly characteristic dockside and crafts workshop atmosphere. It now carries the aura of a gastronomic paradise. In the mid-1920s Lombardi zeroed in on this upcoming characteristic of the neighborhood, and chose wine as the most obvious symbol of the local restaurants and wine-bars. The little wall-fountain in Via della Cisterna is as usual framed in a travertine surround. Resting on a pedestal is a bottle and two wine measures, which spout water into a half-vat. From here the water follows Lombardi's hallmark itinerary, flowing down into the grate in the pavement.

Opposite
*The Books or Sapienza university
fountain in Via degli Staderari.*

Various

This chapter comprises the fountains that caught Francesco Venturi's attention in the course of his dual photographic survey during the summer. The order is more or less chronological, according to each fountain's original configuration.

The fountain at Santa Maria in Trastevere

The fountain was allegedly commissioned by Pope Adrian I (r. 772–795), but actually it was a case of renovating an existing monument from the time of Augustus, and reactivating its supply pipes. During the Middle Ages the fountain largely assumed the form it has today (though it was more set away from the church's facade), and for centuries it offered a model for later fountains.

In modern times the fountain was restored on various occasions, and in 1590–91 it was connected up to the new Acqua Felice system. After being twice interrupted (because the conduits over the Ponte Rotto were damaged by flooding), in 1659 the water supply was switched to the Acqua Paola by order of Alexander VII, who entrusted the fountain's restoration to Gianlorenzo Bernini. Bernini dismantled the old monument and re-erected it at the center of the square, respecting the focal axes of the earlier design.

Following instructions from Innocent XI, in 1694 Carlo Fontana made alterations to Bernini's work: he cleaned and enlarged the basin, and replaced the four shells (containing a spurting head) with those that can be seen today, to ensure the correct proportions with the new lower basin.

In 1873 the original stepped plinth was raised to offer a total of seven steps.

The Fontana della Navicella

During his pontificate, Leo X (r. 1513–21) ordered the substitution of an old fountain fed by water from the Aqua Claudia aqueduct. The fountain outside the church of Santa Maria in Domnica (of which he was the titular cardinal), consists of a small basin containing a rectangular column base bearing up a sculpture of an antique sailing vessel, from which the water falls into the tub below. At the end of the 1500s the Fontana della Navicella, which soon became the name for identifying the area, was fed by the Acqua Felice system. For centuries the little boat faced the church, but when the fountain was restored in 1931 it was turned so that its right flank lies in line with the church's portico.

The Fontana dei Leoni, below the Capitol

In 1564 Pius V bestowed on the Roman people two Egyptian lions carved from a superb pink-veined gray granite that were found in the fourteenth century among the relics in the Campus Martius.

The Conservatori del Comune decided to use them to ennoble the *cordonata* or graded ramp built by Michelangelo. From 1578 to 1583 the two lions commanded the bot-

Opposite and above
Fountain at Santa Maria in Trastevere.

The Navicella or Boat fountain on the
Caelian; one of the lions at the foot of
the Capitol ramp.

Opposite
Details of one of the elaborate
undulating shells from the fountain at
Santa Maria in Trastevere.

Three details from the Pantheon fountain.

tom of the ramp, raised on pedestals bearing the arms of the three Conservatori (Camillo Pignanelli, Marco Santacroce, and Ottavio Crescenzi), and the prior of the Caporioni (Tiberio Massimi).

In 1587–88 water from the Acqua Felice was piped to the Capitol. At this point the sculptor Francesco Scardua carved a fine basin in granite to designs by Battista Rusconi; the bases on which the lions stood were bored through to allow the passage of the water fistulas.

In 1885 the two basins were demolished; the lions were taken to the Museo Capitolino, and gray marble copies installed in their place.

Through the pages of the magazine *Capitolium* in 1954, Carlo Pietrangeli began a campaign for the restoration of the fountains. In 1955 the original lions were returned to their pedestals and resited at the foot of the ramp; the two basins were carefully reconstructed on the basis of drawings, prints, and early photographs.

THE PANTHEON FOUNTAIN

Piazza del Pantheon marks one of the crucial focuses of Christian Rome. In the nineteenth century it has hosted one of the most important street markets of the city, and therefore required a proper fountain of its own. During the pontificate of Eugene IV (r. 1331–47) the piazza was endowed with a large porphyry dish accompanied by two basalt lions (which were later removed by Sixtus V to adorn the new *mostra terminale* of the Acqua Felice aqueduct).

After the rehabilitation of the Acqua Vergine system, the square inherited a fountain designed by Giacomo Della Porta in 1575, which involved reusing the porphyry bowl; this remained in the square until 1740, when it was used for the sarcophagus of Clement XII in the Lateran basilica. Della Porta's concept was a combination of both the round and square fountain models, resulting in a lobate arrangement of semicircles at each side of a square. The construction was commissioned from the Milanese sculptor Leonardo Sormani, who was responsible for the basin in gray African marble and the stepped base. The mascaron water-spouts on the central element, which are flanked by sculpted dolphins, form a set with the other four on the Fontana del Moro in Piazza Navona.

In 1662, by order of the Chigi pope, Alexander VII (r. 1655–67), the slums around the Pantheon were demolished and the pavement level of the square lowered; furthermore, the plinth on which the fountain rested was replaced with a large profiled base with steps.

Some fifty years passed, and in 1711 Clement XI (r. 1700–21) commissioned further improvements in and around the square. The fountain's center was endowed with a sculpted element representing a mossy crag with water-snakes, dolphins, and coats of arms, together with an obelisk (disinterred at the end of the fourteenth century and previously placed in Piazza San Macuto) crowned with a star and cross motif. The rock, dolphins, and Albani insignia sculpted around the obelisk's base are the work of Vincenzo Felici.

In 1880 the fountain was altered again, and the four relief mascarons flanked by dolphins were replaced with copies. More or less during this period the drinking trough alongside the fountain was removed. The most recent restoration projected was concluded in 1992.

THE FOUNTAIN IN PIAZZA COLONNA

The fountain in Piazza Colonna is the work of Giacomo Della Porta, and dates from 1577. In the original project the fountain was supposed to be accompanied by the recumbent statue of the deity known as "Marforio" (now in the courtyard fountain of the Museo Capitolino), an idea that was luckily discarded.

Left
One of the mascaron water-spouts of the Pantheon fountain.

Below
The fountain in Piazza Colonna.

The sculpted basin adorned with sixteen small lion-heads was set into a much larger, circular pool raised on a low stepped base. In 1830 Alessandro Stocchi eliminated the base, reduced the size of the pool, replaced the raised central bowl with the present, much smaller one; the broad lobate basin was embellished at either end with a composition comprising a half-shell and a pair of dolphins.

After the unification of Italy the Montecitorio and Chigi palaces nearby were converted to government use, and the fountain's eventful background seems to typify the constant transformation that has characterized Italian politics down the centuries.

THE FONTANA DELLE TARTARUGHE

In 1580 the owner of Palazzo Mattei successfully applied to have the water from the Aqua Virgo piped to Piazza Giudìa outside his family residence. In exchange he pledged to pave the square and install a fountain for public use.

An existing basin sculpted in antiquity was used for the new fountain, which took many years to complete and was built to designs by Giacomo Della Porta. It may be that the architect was only responsible for the two basins, and over the years the project was repeatedly modified, including the substitution of the white marble statues for two bronze sculptures.

The main tub is delimited by a mixtilinear rim. The central composition comprises four large, bowl-shaped shells in marble, each surmounted by a small dolphin; above these four youths give a helping hand to four small turtles struggling to climb into the top dish of the fountain.

Actually, in 1586 the youths originally bore up dolphins; and in 1637 during alterations their upstretched arms empty for some time. In 1658 Pope Alexander VII decided to entrust the completion to Gianlorenzo Bernini, who restored the existing composition and made the shell bowls more solid. Then he had four little turtles made in his workshop and added to the top dish, which is adorned with putti heads.

In the mid-seventeenth century the Fontana delle Tartarughe, or Turtles fountain, assumed its definitive configuration. In 1940 the turtles and youths were removed to protect them from possible bomb damage, and were not returned until 1948. Recently the entire fountain was restored and the corroded original turtles replaced with copies.

THE FOUNTAIN AT PALAZZO SENATORIO
ON THE CAPITOL

In the mid-sixteenth century, at the height of the Renaissance, the Capitoline hill was extensively remodeled by the great Michelangelo Buonarroti, but the completion of his ambitious scheme was long in coming. Toward the end of the century the reigning pope, Sixtus V, had the Acqua Felice ducts extended from the Madonna dei Monti as far as the Capitol, enabling the creation of a grand fountain in the square crowning the hill.

The fountain, which is set against the double stairway on the main facade of the building, has a very spotted history. After much delay, two basins were installed between a pair of gigantic travertine statues representing river-gods, dating from the first century A.D.; originally from the Baths of Constantine on the Quirinal, Michelangelo had them brought to the Capitol and placed at the steps of the Palazzo Senatorio. The Nile reclines on the left, his left elbow resting on a sphinx and a cornucopia propped up against his shoulder. His counterpart on the right, originally the Tigris, was later adjusted and became the Tiber, and the lion replaced with a she-wolf suckling the twins Romulus and Remus. (In the 1700s the statues and fountain were protected by an enclosure.)

In 1593 a statue of Minerva was installed in the central exedra, but was replaced in 1693 by a statue of the goddess Roma. Until 1720 the goddess was flanked by a pair of gesso "prisons," whose models are on display in the courtyard of the Palazzo dei Conservatori.

The Turtles fountain in Piazza Mattei.

Three details of the Turtles fountain in Piazza Mattei.

PIVS·VII·PONT·MAX·
QVOD·ABSOLVENDVM·SVPERERAT
ADDITO·CRATERE·EXCITATO·SALIENTE
SIMPLEGMA·CONSVMMAVIT
A·D·MDCCCXVIII·PONTIF·XIX·

Opposite, top, and in this page
The fountain in Palazzo Senatorio on the Capitol; the reclining Nile statue.

Opposite, bottom
The fountain at Monte Cavallo, with Castor and Pollux, the horse-tamers.

THE FOUNTAIN AT MONTE CAVALLO (PIAZZA DEL QUIRINALE)

In 1572 Pope Gregory III's attention was drawn to the estate on the Quirinal (started by the Carafa and continued by the Este dynasties), and decided to install a pontifical summer palace on its slopes. By 1585 the new palace was ready and inhabited, and the popes soon began to enjoy its amenities in the summer months.

During the pontificate of Sixtus V the clearing in front of the palace was redeveloped, and with the arrival of piped water via the refurbished Acqua Felice aqueduct, a new fountain was in order.

In 1589 the two gigantic statues of the Dioscuri, Castor and Pollux, were restored and shifted to command the center of the square (whose name Monte Cavallo derives from the two gods' reputation as horse-tamers), their gaze turned to Via Pia. The fountain installed alongside is very simple, with a profiled upper basin resting on an octagonal pedestal; four lion-head waterspouts alternate with the pope's family crest, emitting water down a channel carved into the travertine base.

In 1783 Pius VI (r. 1775–99) had the statues turned to face the Quirinal Palace, their horses looking outward, and made use of the space between the statues to erect an obelisk from the Mausoleum of Augustus. The old fountain was taken to pieces, but not supplanted. In 1818 the pontiff's successor Pius VII (r. 1800–23) ordered the entire monument to be remodeled, and contracted Raffaele Stern as the director of works, who made use of the capacious basin and neat marble bollard and iron railing previously employed in 1593 by Giacomo Della Porta for the fountain in the Campo Vaccino.

One of Rome's most celebrated monumental fountains is therefore actually a triumphant concoction of recycled elements and materials from all ages – ancient Egyptian, late imperial Roman, and modern.

The fountain in Piazza dell'Aracoeli.

THE FOUNTAIN IN PIAZZA DELL'ARACOELI

The area at the foot of the long flight of steps leading down from the church of Santa Maria in Aracoeli, one of Rome's oldest, was once a densely populated, poor neighborhood which was erased during work on the colossal Vittoriano monument (1885–1911), and the opening of Via del Teatro di Marcello. The ancient square was the site of a busy street market, and needed a proper supply of water. To this purpose, in 1589 Giacomo Della Porta (assisted by Andrea Brasca, Pietro Gucci, and Pace Naldini) designed an elongated lobate basin raised on a tiered base surrounded by a channel that collected the water issuing from four lion-head waterspouts. On the upper section four putti poured water from small vessels in their hands.

After the seventeenth-century restoration under Clement XI (r. 1700–21), the channeled base was removed and the fountain was inserted into a circular sunken pool. An enclosure was also erected, consisting of a set of marble bollards with a metal rail; the fountain itself was crowned with the armorial bearings of the reigning pope's family, the Albani.

The extensive urban renewal schemes of the late nineteenth and early twentieth centuries had left the Aracoeli fountain dispossessed, marooned in a rather desolate spot without a point of reference for its proportions, and it became a sort of traffic island hidden behind a swathe of greenery.

THE FOUNTAIN IN PIAZZA CAMPITELLI

The fountain was built in 1589 by Pompilio De Benedetti to designs by Giacomo Della Porta, and paid for by Mario Capizucchi, Giacomo Albertoni, and Giovambattista Riccia, who collectively disbursed 300 *scudi* to have it erected outside their town mansions overlooking the square.

The Monte Cavallo fountain, seen against the Quirinal Palace.

The fountain in Piazza Campitelli,
with detail of the central element.

Opposite
The fountain in Campo de' Fiori; the
Marforio fountain in the courtyard of
the Museo Capitolino.

Detail of the colossal reclining figure of Marforio.

The fountain originally stood closer to the church of Santa Maria Campitelli; when this was enlarged in 1675–79, however, the fountain was moved to its present site.

On a sculpted octagonal base stands a travertine basin with a tablet bearing the insignia of the Roman senate, profiled to match the base; other decorations on the basin include six separate escutcheons and two sculpted masks by Della Porta. At the center of the basin the water spills out of a sort of marble chalice decorated with festoons.

Over the years the fountain has been restored several times, and in the 1900s alterations were made by Raffaele De Vico.

THE FOUNTAIN IN CAMPO DE' FIORI

In the fifteenth century the square known as Campo de' Fiori (literally, Field of Flowers) became one of the city's most vital focuses of daily trade, and was thronged with countless merchants and craftsmen (as can be inferred from the names of the surrounding streets), together with the horse-market held on Mondays and Saturdays, and a steady flow of visitors and pilgrims, whence the high concentration of *osterie*, taverns, and guest houses. The sheer congestion of all this daily business in the square made a proper water supply essential, even as early as the 1400s.

Much later, in 1590, the square saw the installation of a new fountain with an elliptical pool embellished with four bronze dolphins and a marble basin at its center. At some point the entire unit was sunk into the pavement to facilitate the flow of the gravity water supply, as the pressure of the Acqua Vergine was particularly weak in the Regola and Parione wards, despite improvements to the conduits.

However, the site was so busy that the fountain's basin was often cluttered with litter and other assorted refuse, impeding its proper use, so in 1621 it was provided with a lid that made it resemble a huge soup tureen.

In 1889, during work on the new monument to the sixteenth-century philosopher Giordano Bruno, the Tureen fountain was dismantled and packed away in the municipal storerooms (not to be recomposed until 1924, in the square before the Chiesa Nuova). In 1898 the regular market in Piazza Navona was transferred to Campo de' Fiori, necessitating a new fountain. The site of the original fountain was occupied, however, by the statue to Bruno, a "martyr to free thinking," and so the new unit was installed on the west side of the square. A stepped base and plinth support an oval pool at whose center rises an elliptical lobate basin resembling a tureen. The water issues from a central spout and from a patera in each of the four extremities, alternating with carved imitation ring-handles.

THE FONTANA DEL MARFORIO ON THE CAPITOL

In 1594 the municipal authorities decided to build a fountain using the colossal first-century statue of a river-god, later dubbed Marforio, one of Rome's notorious "talking" statues to which, together with his partner Pasquino, anonymous written comments of a satirical (and often pungently critical) nature were attached. The statue was coupled with a marine dragon, and the composition assembled in a pool.

The Capitoline fountain was attached to the retaining wall of the terracing beside the church of Santa Maria d'Aracoeli, and was conceived to provide an architectural counterpoint in the square, which at the time was lacking the building that now houses the Museo Capitolino. The fountain was enclosed in a small triumphal arch composition of two superimposed orders. The fountain stood on a rocky formation in the arches of the lower order, where the two-tailed sea-monster poured water into the basin, perhaps trilobate; the upper order was graced with two statues, coats of arms, ornamental compositions of coquillages and heads, together with other bas-relief designs. The entire arrangement was crowned with a broken pediment.

The fountain was demolished in 1650, upon the completion of the building now housing the museum. After several temporary solutions, under Clement XII (r. 1730–40) a new fountain was installed in the courtyard of the new palazzo. In 1734 the statue and two columns were set up in a niche, surmounted by a marble tablet. Despite the handsome neoclassical backdrop, the new fountain had less depth than its predecessor, and the recumbent statue a less monumental setting. The fountain's basin is shallow and is filled from a splayed jet of water issuing from the head of a two-tailed dolphin.

THE FONTANA DEL FACCHINO IN VIA LATA

The Fontana del Facchino or Porter's fountain was probably built in 1588–98, and formerly stood in Via del Corso, with a larger basin, framed in an aedicule.

In the mid-1600s the entire area was commonly known as the Isola del Facchino. Around 1720 a certain Livio De Carolis commissioned the design and construction of a new town residence from the architect Alessandro Specchi, who returned the fountain to its original site.

In 1874 it was transferred to a more decorous position in nearby Via Lata, and its architectural surround was reduced in size. It is evident that the statue does not in fact portray a porter or caddie, but rather an *acquarolo*, one of the notoriously surly water-bearers who took water to the garrets on the upper floors of the apartment blocks. The attribution of the fountain's design to Michelangelo is undoubtedly spurious.

The Water-carrier wall-fountain in Via Lata.

THE FOUNTAIN AT SANTA MARIA MAGGIORE

The Perretti pope, Sixtus V (r. 1585–90), possessed various properties in the basilica's vicinity, and envisaged a scheme whose focal point was the house of worship on the Esquiline at the center of a network of streets, both old and new. The obelisk became a striking landmark visible along the Via Felice thoroughfare and Via Panisperna. Via Merulana and the continuation of Via Felice connect the church square with the basilicas of Santa Croce and San Giovanni in Laterano.

The zone's new importance as a central part of the city inevitably obliged the authorities to provide a proper supply of running water from the Acqua Felice aqueduct.

In 1615 Carlo Maderno (and his assistant Gaspare de' Vecchi) built a fountain at the foot of a column raised by Maderno in front of the main facade of the church; the new monument may have supplanted an existing medieval fountain that was fed by the Acqua Marcia aqueduct.

The new fountain was composed of an oblong sculpted basin raised on a four-stepped base. In the middle of the basin rose a profiled pedestal crowned with a round basin from which the water flowed.

Early photographs reveal the existence of a drinking trough on the opposite side of the column; restoration work canceled the dragons and eagles of the Borghese house.

THE FONTANA DELLA BARCACCIA

In 1626 Pietro Bernini, the architect behind the Acqua Vergine, designed a new fountain for Piazza di Spagna. For his efforts he received various settlements over the period 1627–29. The day before the last payment for the job in question, Bernini died, and his son Gianlorenzo succeeded him as chief engineer of the Acqua Vergine aqueduct. Gianlorenzo Bernini completed the fountain in three years, conforming with the design proposed by his father: a half-submerged vessel, slightly lower than the level of the pavement.

The prow and poop of the vessel are identical, enabling an ideal symmetry. Two devices of Urban VIII (Barberini) were emblazoned on each end of the vessel, while on the inside

From top
The fountain at Santa Maria Maggiore; the Barcaccia fountain seen from above; detail of the sun-head water-spout inside the ship's hull.

Opposite
Another view of the Barcaccia fountain, toward the Keats-Shelley Memorial House.

at either end two sun-shaped spouts discharge water inward toward the center; two other water jets have since been positioned at either side of the Barberini coats of arms.

Over the years, various ideas regarding the possible formal and symbolic meanings of the boat have been put forward, and the architect's choice of motif is evidently tied to a specific technical strategy. The design of the vessel made it possible to set the fountain below the pavement level so as to get round the problem of low water pressure. At the same time, the idea was perhaps borrowed from the Navicella fountain outside the church of Santa Maria in Domnica; furthermore, Bernini's father built a similar fountain for the foreshore at Naples. For many years the fountain was attributed to Gianlorenzo, whose contribution at most was to work alongside, as his father's assistant.

Thanks to the fountain's position, standing out against the magnificent flight of steps up to the church of Trinità dei Monti, the Barcaccia fountain is a frequent gathering point, and firework displays are often held there.

In the early 1800s, the architect who masterminded the remodeling of nearby Piazza del Popolo, Giuseppe Valadier, tendered a design for the improvement of the water supply and for repaving the square, but it was not until 1888 that the municipal authorities actually implemented the refurbishment of the conduits.

The fountain was disregarded for nearly a century, and has only recently been completely overhauled, with broken parts replaced and the pool made waterproof once more.

THE FONTANA DEL TRITONE

In the year 1625 Cardinal Francesco Barberini bought the Sforza family's villa, which was adjacent to Via Pia and Via Felice, and made a gift of it to his brother Matteo. The new owner promptly proceeded to build a sumptuous dynastic residence upon its grounds, which soon became the symbol of the "papal" family's political and economic prowess.

The main entrance gives onto Via delle Quattro Fontane, while only the left wing of the building borders the piazza, where in 1642–43 Gianlorenzo Bernini installed the Triton fountain. The new monument (restored in 1986–87) was built to glorify the name of the ruling pope (Urban VIII, r. 1623–44), and is based on a clever allegory in honor of the family's triumphs. At the center of a low, broad basin four dolphins bear up a huge open scallop shell with their tails, upon which rides an athletic triton figure carrying a nautilus shell on his head, from which spurts a powerful jet of water.

Admittedly, the fountain's design is an ingenious assemblage of ideas culled from other works, but it earned Bernini everlasting fame. This jewel of a fountain adorns a somewhat secondary site at the side of Palazzo Barberini, at the outer edge of the old city center, in an area that was formerly virtually pasture. With the opening of Via del Tritone, Via Barberini, and Via Veneto, the square became a hub of intense traffic, whereas in the 1870s Piazza Barberini was still considered a sleepy outskirt on the fringes of the baroque quarter, bordered by low houses, stables, and barns.

THE FOUNTAIN AT PALAZZO ANTAMORO

In the period 1667–69 the papal architect Gianlorenzo Bernini built a wall-fountain in the courtyard of the palazzo in Via della Panetteria, owned by one Paolo Strada (the secret chamberlain of Pope Clement IX), to whom the pontiff had donated three *once* of the Acqua Felice supply. For this fountain, Bernini used three of his stock motifs, namely scallop shells, dolphins, and tritons.

In the 1700s the Antamoro counts bought Strada's mansion, which stands in the shadow of the Quirinal Palace. They made alterations to the fountain, substituting their own family coat of arms for the Rospigliosi device, which the original owner had applied as a sign of devotion and fidelity to his patron the pope. A recent restoration project has successfully re-established the former splendor of this little masterpiece.

Details of the Barcaccia and of the Triton fountain.

On pages 177–179
Three views of the Triton fountain and it muscular central figure blowing water out of a huge shell.

THE FOUNTAIN AT PALAZZO SANTACROCE

The construction of the urban mansion of the Santacroce family lasted from the late sixteenth to the mid-seventeenth centuries, and it was erected in the Regola ward opposite the church of San Carlo ai Catinari. The palazzo was bought in the early 1900s and restored by the Pasolini dell'Onda, from Emilia-Romagna.

In the small courtyard within the palace stands a fountain commissioned by the Santacroce, consisting of a bold aedicule with Doric columns and telamons, and a large niche which harbors a statue of Venus on the half-shell, showered with water and surrounded by putti. Below, a large basin is punctuated by water-jets.

THE NYMPHAEUM AT PALAZZO BORGHESE

In the heart of the Palazzo Borghese – whose characteristic shape earned it the appellation "The harpsichord of Rome" – lies a court arcaded on two superimposed orders with twin columns surrounding a *nymphaeum*. Attached to the wall around the garden are three niche-fountains, the central one of which represents the *Bath of Venus*, and the other two *Flora* and *Diana* respectively.

In the late 1600s, in this garden two architects composed one of the most sublime creations of baroque. Gian Paolo Schor and Carlo Rainaldi successfully wed the element of water with an architectural and sculptural setting of remarkable flair and an extensive use of stucco. The device completed the Borghese *reggia*, the pivot of the "Borghese quarter" which revolutionized the layout of part of the Campus Martius ward.

THE FOUNTAIN AT SANTA MARIA IN COSMEDIN

The sixth-century diaconal church of Santa Maria in Cosmedin was extensively reworked in the twelfth century, with the addition of an elegant Romanesque belfry and portico. Successively, it received no further attention, however, and was neglected until the 1700s, when alterations were made to the square. Later, in 1717–19, Pope Clement XI Albani (r. 1700–21) entrusted the remodeling of the square and the construction of a fountain to the Perugia-born architect Carlo Bizzaccheri.

The architect designed an ample octagonal basin with a concave brim, thus forming an eight-pointed star, like the one featured in the Albani coat of arms. The same motif is repeated on the plinth, which is encircled by a wider base enclosed in seven low bollards joined with an iron railing.

The fountain's centerpiece is dominated by two tritons leaning on a craggy travertine boulder bedecked with waterweeds. The tritons are addorsed, that is, facing away from each other and hold up a second basin in the form of a sea-shell sculpted with three small mounds bearing the armorial star of the Albani. The boulder group is the work of Filippo Bai, and the tritons of Francesco Moratti.

Originally, four mascaron spouts adorned the fountain, but they were removed due to the poor delivery capacity of the conduits. Adjoining the fountain the architect installed a water-pump, which was later moved during work on Via del Mare to a new position under the pines of the Lungotevere Aventino.

THE WATER CLOCK

In the courtyard of the town house built by Guglielmo di Vulci in Via del Gesù 62 stands a charming "hydrochronometer" or water clock, dated 1870, inserted in an architectural setting with caryatid-pilasters, antique busts, and a small vase.

Preceding pages
The wall-fountain in the courtyard of Palazzo Antamoro; the niche fountain of Palazzo Santacroce (now Palazzo Pasolini dell'Onda).

Opposite
Detail of the nymphaeum at Palazzo Borghese.

THE FOUNTAIN IN PIAZZA DEI QUIRITI

In 1926 the architect Attilio Selva won a municipal competition for the design of a fountain to be sited in Piazza dei Quiriti. The ideas of this classicizing composition are liberally borrowed from other fountains around the city. The fountain caused a stir when it was first unveiled, as in this case the *quirites* or citizens of ancient Rome, are in fact maidens playing the role of caryatids (distinctly female, but uncommonly muscular), inviting comments in the wry humor so characteristic of Rome, such as: "E te credo che li Romani antichi dovevano fa' sempre la guera, co' ste stangone forzute!" ("With brawny women like that, I'm not surprised the ancient Romans were always at war!").

Rising from the pool set into the ground is a composite baluster surmounted by a convex – not concave – basin out of which spills a steady curtain of water. At its center the four kneeling viragos bear up a lobate bowl from which emerges a pine-cone on a short pedestal; from here the water spurts triumphantly skyward.

Encircled by the tall trees of the Prati quarter, the fountain represents the style of the city when it was the capital of the Kingdom of Italy under the Piedmontese sovereign of the House of Savoy.

Two contrasting views of the fountain at Santa Maria in Cosmedin.

THE "MASCHERONE" AT SANTA SABINA

The eye-catching wall-fountain at the church of Santa Sabina is actually a vestige of one of Rome's characteristic "ballerina" fountains. At the close of the sixteenth century Giacomo Della Porta created one of his most charming, yet least fortunate, architectural fountains. It was built for the Campo Vaccino (the "modern-day" name for the ancient Roman forums): behind a large circular granite basin he arranged a backing with volutes at either side; for the central motif he devised a carved composition consisting of a mascaron on a half-shell.

In no time the fountain – frequently used as a drinking trough – deteriorated and became overgrown. In 1818 the tub was taken to Monte Cavallo (the crossroads at the Quirinal Palace) and united with the obelisk and towering horse-tamer statues of Castor and Pollux. The sculpted mask was affixed to the fountain at the Porto Leonino wharf which Leo XII (r. 1823–29) had had rehabilitated, on the right bank of the Tiber in front of San Giovanni de' Fiorentini, the church commissioned by the Florentine colony of Rome in the early sixteenth century.

The walling-in of the Tiber and the creation of the embankment avenues hastened the demise of the riverside ports, and the fountain was demolished around 1890. In 1936 the mascaron, after a lengthy spell in the municipal warehouses, was transferred to the Aventine, to a spot near the church of Santa Sabina, and mounted above an antique granite bathtub on a wall in the little park known as the Parco Savello.

THE FONTANA DEL SENATO AT SANT'EUSTACHIO

The so-called Senate fountain embodies two characteristics of the fountains of Rome, namely, the multiple reuse of material from the past, and the progressive expropriation of the once much lived-in inner-city quarters by the ever-burgeoning governmental departments of the capital, the "political citadel," as it were.

The amebic growth of this citadel and the creeping expansion of the area occupied by the offices of the Senate have steadily transformed this sector of the city, in an ongoing development program in which various historical buildings have been annexed to Palazzo Madama (the home of the Senate), and a huge tunnel has been driven beneath the entire block. In the course of this urban renewal program a large circular basin carved in red granite was discovered, originally from the Baths of Nero (which once occupied most of this area), and in 1987 it was installed in the square as a new fountain.

The Water Clock in the courtyard of Palazzo Guglielmi; the fountain in Piazza dei Quiriti.

BIBLIOGRAPHICAL NOTE

The historical and literary coverage of the subject of the water supply, aqueducts, and fountains of Rome is vast. In order to avoid an overlong and ultimately impractical bibliography, here follows a brief list of significant available recent publications; each one contains a detailed bibliography of relevant works on the subject.

Various, *Il trionfo dell'acqua. Acque e acquedotti a Roma. IV sec. a.C.–XX sec. d.C.* Rome 1986.
Various, *L'uomo e l'acqua.* Rome 1990.
Coppa, C., et al., *Acque e acquedotti a Roma, 1870–1984.* Rome 1984.
Pace, P., *Gli acquedotti a Roma.* Rome 1983.

Brizzi, B., *Le fontane di Roma.* Rome 1987.
Candelori, A., Somigli, D., *Le fontane di Roma.* Rome 1989.
D'Onofrio, C., *Le fontane di Roma.* Rome 1986.

A new publication, *Le fontane di Roma*, by W. Pocino was published while this book was still being prepared; a pity, as it would have saved me a great deal of trouble.

M. S.

The Senate fountain at Sant'Eustachio.

Opposite
The Mascherone wall-fountain at Santa Sabina.

INDEX

Aqueducts, ancient

Aqueducts, modern

Artists & Architects

Emblems

Popes

Printed and bound by
Amilcare Pizzi S.p.A. arti grafiche
Cinisello Balsamo (Milan)

September 1996